NATHANIEL HAWTHORNE
The Introduction of an American Author's Work into Japan

ESSEX INSTITUTE HISTORICAL COLLECTIONS
July 1993 · VOL. 129, NO. 3

Published by the Peabody Essex Museum

Oil portrait of Nathaniel Hawthorne (1804–64) by Charles Osgood (1809–90). Oil on canvas, 1840.

ISSN 0014–0953

Essex Institute Historical Collections

Issued Quarterly by the Peabody Essex Museum

VOL. 129 JULY 1993 NO. 3

The established texts of "David Swan" and "Fancy's Show Box," the first two Hawthorne short stories to be translated into Japanese, appear courtesy of the Centenary Edition of the Works of Nathaniel Hawthorne published by the Ohio State University Center for Textual Studies (Columbus, Ohio: Ohio State University Press, 1974). These stories are included in volume nine of the series, *Twice-told Tales,* pages 183–90 and 220–26, respectively.

Lithograph of Nathaniel Hawthorne by J. E. Baker for Armstrong & Co., Boston, Mass.

Preface

GIVEN the astounding popularity of Nathaniel Hawthorne in Japan, an extremely active collaboration between Japanese and American scholars has developed. One clear illustration of this is the existence of the Nathaniel Hawthorne Society of Japan. This association was founded on 17 October 1981 in Tokyo, just seven years after its American counterpart was created in New York City.[1]

A close working relationship between the Nathaniel Hawthorne Society of Japan and the Peabody Essex Museum was initiated on 17 July 1989 by a letter from Professor Fumio Ano (a founding member of the society) to Anne Farnam, president of the Essex Institute. Knowing of my keen interest in Japan and my regular schedule of trips there, she referred me to Professor Ano in the summer of that year with a view to establishing the groundwork for joint projects. I soon met with Professor Nathaniel Hagiwara of Senshu University in Tokyo, who was then secretary-general of the society, to further these objectives. Almost from the outset of our discussions, we envisioned a Hawthorne exhibition in Japan as well as the publication of material by Japanese Hawthorne scholars in the *Essex Institute Historical Collections*. A succession of meetings took place in 1990 and 1991 that paved the way for the developments that we sought, and, in April of 1991, I had the great privilege of addressing the Tokyo Salon of the Nathaniel Hawthorne Society of Japan.

By May 1991, we had arrived at a publication plan in which Professor

1. The Japanese society commenced with fifty-two founding members, expanding to eighty-one members by the time of its first annual conference, and presently consists of 240 individuals. Jukichi Suzuki served as its first president from October 1981 through April 1991. Aiko Moro'oka then assumed the post from May 1991 to April 1993. Most recently, Tadatoshi Saito was elected to this position as of May 1993. The society presently has two chapters: the Tokyo Salon and the Sendai Symposium. The Tokyo branch meets five times per year, while the Sendai group holds between eight and ten meetings during the year.

The Nathaniel Hawthorne Society of Japan began its publishing activities with an annual newsletter in 1982, establishing an editorial office at Tohoku University in Sendai; in 1987, this office was moved to Senshu University in Tokyo. The ninth and final issue of the newsletter was printed in 1990, due to the expectation that the scope of the publication would be expanded to include full-scale articles in a new medium entitled *Forum*, published for the first time in 1991. The second issue followed in 1993.

Ano was invited to produce an article on the introduction of Hawthorne's writings into Japan during the Meiji period. To balance such a piece, Professor David Cody (now at Hartwick College) was solicited to review—from the perspective of an American professor—the recent Hawthorne studies written in Japan. Progress continued on this mutual enterprise in 1991 and 1992, with meetings both in Salem and Japan. In June of 1992, the conference of the Nathaniel Hawthorne Society in Concord, Massachusetts, provided the opportunity for Professor Ano and his daughter Reiko (herself a student of Hawthorne) to visit the Salem area and settle many of the details of the article that he was writing.

This Salem visit coincided with that of Mr. Ryoku Kato, curator of the Folk Museum of Ota Borough in Tokyo, who was then planning a major exhibit on the history of Salem, utilizing rare books, manuscripts, and artifacts from the collections of the Peabody Essex Museum. The dialogue between Professor Ano and Mr. Kato ultimately led to the inclusion of a special Hawthorne section in the Ota Borough exhibit, thus bringing to fruition the second component of our original strategy. Professor Ano assisted Mr. Kato in the preparation of this portion of the exhibit, which opened on 15 May 1993, and also delivered a lecture at the Folk Museum of Ota Borough on the subject of Hawthorne on 6 June. In addition, Professor Ano helped in the creation of the catalogue for the Ota Borough exhibit and, in particular, its Hawthorne segment.

In the last phase of these publishing endeavors, I had the good fortune to make the acquaintance of Mr. Yōji Suzuki, who is the librarian of the Maruzen Library of Books on Books. He was invaluable in my attempt to characterize how Western-language books were imported into Meiji Japan. His firm generously provided data and images that made it possible to document the means of this importation. This is indicative of the seemingly boundless cooperation that the Peabody Essex Museum has encountered from the Nathaniel Hawthorne societies of both Japan and the United States, the Folk Museum of Ota Borough, and the Maruzen Company. We offer this publication in recognition of the extraordinary camaraderie demonstrated by these organizations.

FREDERIC A. SHARF

The Origins of the Distribution of Western Books in Meiji Japan

By FREDERIC A. SHARF*

JAPAN officially opened to the Western world on 1 July 1859. The Japanese government had created at Yokohama a completely new city that was to serve as the primary location of Western merchants and a place of nurture for the various aspects of Western culture, technology, and life-style that the Japanese felt they needed to adopt.

Prior to these developments in Yokohama, Japanese contact with the West had been entirely confined to Nagasaki, where Dutch merchants maintained a trading base. The Dutch language thereby became the crucial medium of absorbing Western thought. In Yokohama, however, all commercial transactions were conducted in English, and it became obvious to the Japanese that Dutch was no longer an acceptable language for international communication. To ease the transition, the Yokohama foreign merchants made English-Dutch dictionaries available to the Japanese so that those proficient in Dutch were soon able to adapt their language skills to function in English. It became apparent to the Japanese intelligentsia, however, that a genuine understanding of the West could only be obtained through the vehicle of Western books. The merchants at Nagasaki had provided some access to Western books, but there had been no concerted effort to import such items.

*Frederic A. Sharf is president of the Sharf Marketing Group and a specialist in Meiji-period prints and photography. He would like to express his appreciation to Yōji Suzuki, the director of the Maruzen Library of Books on Books and the Maruzen Company archives. Mr. Suzuki was extremely helpful in supplying much of the data pertaining to Maruzen's publishing history. He also provided a privately printed essay by Professor Sugiyama of Tokyo Keizai University entitled "Enlightenment and Nationalism: 'Maruzen' in Its Earliest Days." This essay was presented at the University of London on 3 May 1989 at the School of Asian and African Studies.

Professor Fumio Ano of Tohoku University also contributed to the author's understanding of the introduction of Western books into Japan by translating sections of Maruzen's own three-volume company history *(One Hundred Years of Maruzen: With the Progress of the Modernization of Japan)* published in Tokyo in 1980.

The man largely responsible for organizing access to Western books in Japan was Yukichi Fukuzawa. He had learned Dutch as a young man and was a vocal supporter of Westernization. He ran a private school that disseminated Western traditions to students embracing the new social order of Meiji Japan. One of the first Japanese to purchase an English-Dutch dictionary, he became one of the first Japanese to become fluent in English.

When the Tokugawa government organized the first Japanese foreign embassy (which traveled to the United States in 1860), Fukuzawa was selected to accompany the delegation as far as San Francisco. While there, Fukuzawa and one of his companions each purchased an edition of Webster's dictionary—the first copies of this seminal work to reach Japan. In 1862, Fukuzawa was chosen as a member of the first Japanese embassy to visit Europe. For this trip, the Tokugawa government provided each participant with a personal spending allowance. Fukuzawa spent most of his funds purchasing books in London, and this constituted the first real importation of English books into Japan. Fukuzawa was also a member of a diplomatic mission that journeyed to Washington, D.C., and New York City in 1867. His travel allowance was now considerably larger, and he was able to buy a substantial quantity of Western books. When he returned to Yokohama in June of that year, these printed materials were temporarily impounded by a suspicious team of customs inspectors who had never seen such a large shipment of foreign books.

By the fall of 1867, the books that Fukuzawa had brought back from the United States were available to students in his private school in Tokyo. Instead of a student having access to a single copy of a book in English from which he was expected to transcribe a personal copy, Fukuzawa was able to permit his students to work directly from an original printed book, since he had obtained multiple copies of those items that he felt were important for didactic purposes. One of the most notable of these educational tools was *Peter Parley's Universal History* (the first edition of which was written by Nathaniel Hawthorne and published in Boston in 1837).

Fukuzawa's school was located in a section of Tokyo known as Tsukiji that the Japanese government had specifically designated as a foreign concession, that is, a place where foreigners could reside while visiting or conducting business in Tokyo. The space available to Fukuzawa in Tsukiji was limited, while the demand for his services increased rapidly. As a consequence, he relocated his school in 1868 (the first year of the Meiji era) to more spacious premises in Shiba, and in the process changed its name to Keio Gijuku; in 1871, he moved the school to an even larger site in Mita, the present location of Keio University. This rapid growth in Fukuzawa's operation may be cited as evidence of the Western influence that was revolutionizing the educational world of Japan.

In 1867, Dr. Yuteki Hayashi, a physician in Yokohama, decided to become a student at Fukuzawa's Tokyo school while continuing his medical practice. Since there was no train service from Yokohama to Tokyo at that time, the eighteen-mile journey must have been arduous and time-consuming. It certainly was testimony to the strong commitment that Hayashi had for further education and, in particular, the study of English.

Although Fukuzawa was only two years older than Hayashi, he already commanded great respect because of his extensive travel and knowledge of the West. Fukuzawa functioned as the mentor who suggested to Hayashi the need for an organized, commercial enterprise for the importation of Western books. Hayashi responded to this challenge by renting a small house in Yokohama in 1868 where he began dealing in secondhand Japanese books and in Western books as well. This business was operated under the name of Z. P. Maruya.

It seems clear that the support and patronage of Fukuzawa were major factors behind the success of Hayashi. Fukuzawa records in his autobiography that in 1868 one of his colleagues purchased a used copy of Francis Wayland's *The Elements of Moral Science*.[1] Fukuzawa determined that this work would be very useful for his students and placed an order with Maruya for sixty copies. The firm would become renowned for its ability to meet the emerging demand for multiple copies of books.

1. Yukichi Fukuzawa, *The Autobiography of Fukuzawa Yukichi,* trans. Eiichi Kiyooka (Tokyo: Hokuseido Press, 1981), 70 (appendix).

The initial success of the Maruya venture prompted its organizers to create a joint stock company using the same name, and this was officially launched on 1 January 1869. The concept of establishing a joint stock enterprise was almost certainly the inspiration of Fukuzawa.

The tenets to which Fukuzawa subscribed led him to conclude that Japan needed to train successful businessmen who would become independent operators as opposed to intermediaries with Western merchants. He believed that as long as foreign agents controlled trade, Japan would never be able to achieve true equality in the eyes of the West. Fukuzawa adhered so strongly to this conviction that the Japanese must develop Western business skills that in 1873 he made available in Japanese translation Bryant and Stratton's *Common School Bookkeeping*. In 1875, he became one of the organizers of the first commercial school in Japan. One needs to view the initiation and development of the Maruya business of importing foreign books both in its educational context and as an integral part of Japan's clear objective of attaining equality as a participant in international trade.

Hayashi's business under the Maruya name quickly prospered. In 1870, the main office was moved to Tokyo, which had emerged as the major city of Meiji Japan. In 1871, a branch office was opened in Osaka. By 1872, there was one in Kyoto and another in Nagoya in 1874. With this distribution network in place, Western books were made available to the major marketplaces of Meiji Japan. Hayashi decided, having had this level of progress assured, that his expanding chain needed a presence in the Kanda section of Tokyo—a district regarded as the center for the publishing industry. Fully cognizant of its literary tradition, Hayashi unveiled in 1881 a Western-style retail bookstore under the name of Nakanishiya.

At the outset, the Maruya operation purchased books through the established Yokohama companies, but, as early as 1872, direct trading connections were created with the United States. By 1874, comparable relations with England were in place. It can be documented that by 1880 Maruya was a substantial customer of George Bell & Sons of London, the publishers of both Bohn's Standard Library volumes and Bohn's Cheap Series of Standard Works. Large quantities of books from these series were being imported into Japan, including the novels

Photograph of the Nakanishiya store dating from approximately 1887. It was supplied courtesy of the Maruzen Company.

of Hawthorne. (For more information on the importation of books into Meiji Japan, see the Appendix at the conclusion of this article.)

Maruya's business activity was so considerable that it warranted the publication of a printed catalogue in 1880, listing the various titles available. This catalogue was printed in English, as were subsequent editions in 1883, 1885, 1888, 1890, and 1900. In 1897, the company began publishing a monthly magazine entitled *Gakuto* (subtitled the *Beacon Light of Learning*) that targeted the academic and scholarly market. While this publication was in the format of a monthly journal that carried articles, it was functionally an advertising medium with many notices of the various books recently imported.

There never was any real person named Zenpachi P. Maruya. Hayashi had selected the name for symbolic purposes; the Japanese characters that form the name could also be interpreted as meaning "worldwide," and this strategy was a part of his business concept from the start. His commercial success was so great, however, that he was

大正四年七月五日發行　毎月二回五日・二十日發行　明治三十年三月十八日內務省許可

From HISTORY OF ENGLISH GLASS-PAINTINGS

第十九年七月號

丸善株式會社

Cover of the July 1915 issue of *Gakuto,* a magazine published by Maruzen Company, Ltd. The photograph appears courtesy of Professor David Cody.

Cover of number ten of the thirty-fourth volume of *Gakuto,* a magazine published by Maruzen Company, Ltd. The photograph appears courtesy of Professor David Cody.

An image taken from a book entitled *Tokyo Syoko-e Hakuran-e (The Picture Album of Commercial and Industrial Houses in Tokyo)*. The volume was published in May of 1885. The Tokyo store of the Maruzen Company is depicted at this period. The photograph used for reproduction was supplied courtesy of the company.

induced to register the name Maruya as his personal name, and among his employees the business name of Zenpachi P. Maruya became shortened to Maruzen. This transitional process reached a culmination in 1893 when a new limited company, incorporated according to classic Western business procedures, was established under the name of Maruzen, the same firm that exists today.

In discussing the means by which Fukuzawa and Hayashi introduced the business of importing Western books to Meiji Japan, we must also recognize that there were other channels through which such books arrived during this period. There were, for example, numerous foreign employees of the Meiji government who brought personal libraries with them and who had books sent to them during their stay in Japan. The Japanese government was also becoming very aggressive in sponsoring students in many other countries, but especially the United States and Great Britain. Such students returned with their own personal collections, and afterwards doubtless ordered books from publishers in the countries where they had studied.

Perhaps the most significant source of Western books, outside of the Maruya business distribution, was the large group of English and American missionaries who started arriving in Japan in 1859. They routinely set up schools for teaching English as an aspect of their religious mission. In the early years, this was the major dimension of their missionary activities insofar as they were prohibited from officially promoting Christianity until 1873. Missionaries had a vested interest in making books in English available to the Japanese, since it was their hope that if the Japanese learned English they might better absorb Christianity. The missionaries not only brought books with them; their students in Japan clearly looked to them for a continuing supply, and books were sent from various publishers directly to converted Japanese.

The works of Nathaniel Hawthorne were especially well suited to the goals of the missionary agenda. They could be read as a means of learning rudimentary world history (*Peter Parley's Universal History* was definitely chosen for this purpose). They could also be utilized as English reading lessons (his stories were included in such series as *Swinton's Reader*). Even the missionary activities could benefit from the works of Hawthorne since they could be construed to be suffused with a morality that was essentially Christian. The following excerpts, taken from a letter of the Reverend John Hyde DeForest to his friends at the Yale Divinity School, illustrate the impact of *Peter Parley's Universal History* on Japanese readers:

> Japan is intensely earnest in the study of modern sciences, and that through the English language. . . . Japan has at last formally adopted English as the one to be taught in her schools and used as widely as possible in her public offices. I regard this as a most providential step in Christianizing this empire. The English language is saturated with Christian thought. Peter Parley never could have had the remotest idea that his simple "Universal History" would be one of the means of spreading the Jesus Way in this far-off nation. . . . A physician recently baptized here, said to me the other day, "The reason my friend the lawyer doesn't become a Christian is because he doesn't know history. If he could read Parley, he would have something to build on." . . . It must be confessed that Parley is one of our active missionaries. Some two months ago, while spending a night a hundred miles from here in

> a hotel, two or three of us were talking together about Christianity. . . . Our words were heard by the young fellow who had the adjoining room. . . . We invited him to come right into our circle . . . in the course of the talk he asked me the difference between *Lord* and *God.* I found he had learned the words from Parley's history.[2]

One of the leaders of the missionary community, which was headquartered in Yokohama, was an American medical doctor and educator named James Curtis Hepburn. He arrived in Japan in 1859 and by 1867 he was able to publish the first comprehensive Japanese-English dictionary. This became an essential tool for many foreigners working in Japan and certainly for Japanese students. An important parallel project for the missionaries was the publication of the Bible in Japanese. The first section of the New Testament, the Gospel of Matthew, became available in 1871, and the entire New Testament was completed in 1879. The Old Testament, however, was not translated until 1887.

Works of literature in English were introduced into Meiji Japan with a multitude of purposes in mind. While one could argue, for example, that their primary function was as exercise books for the learning of the language, they also were serving to attune the Japanese to Western thought and technology with a view to attaining an equal standing in the community of nations, as the following comments from a letter of Ume Tsuda, a Japanese educator, to Mrs. Charles Lanman suggest:

> I want to ask Mr. Lanman if he would ask one of the leading publishing firms of New York or Boston to send me regularly the lists of their new book publications, that is, of school books. He could say that I am the head teacher in English in the Empress' [*sic*] school for the daughters of nobles, and that school books that may be required will be ordered from America directly, and that I want to keep a list of all their new publications. I suppose, they might from time to time send some sample books to look at, too. I want, just at present, a good grammar and something in the way of a reader. I have thought a good standard story book, not too difficult, something written for children, would give a better idea

2. This letter was dated 18 January 1886 and was printed in *The Evolution of a Missionary: A Biography of John Hyde DeForest* (New York: Fleming H. Revell, 1914). The quoted passages may be found on pages 137 and 138 of this book by Charlotte B. DeForest.

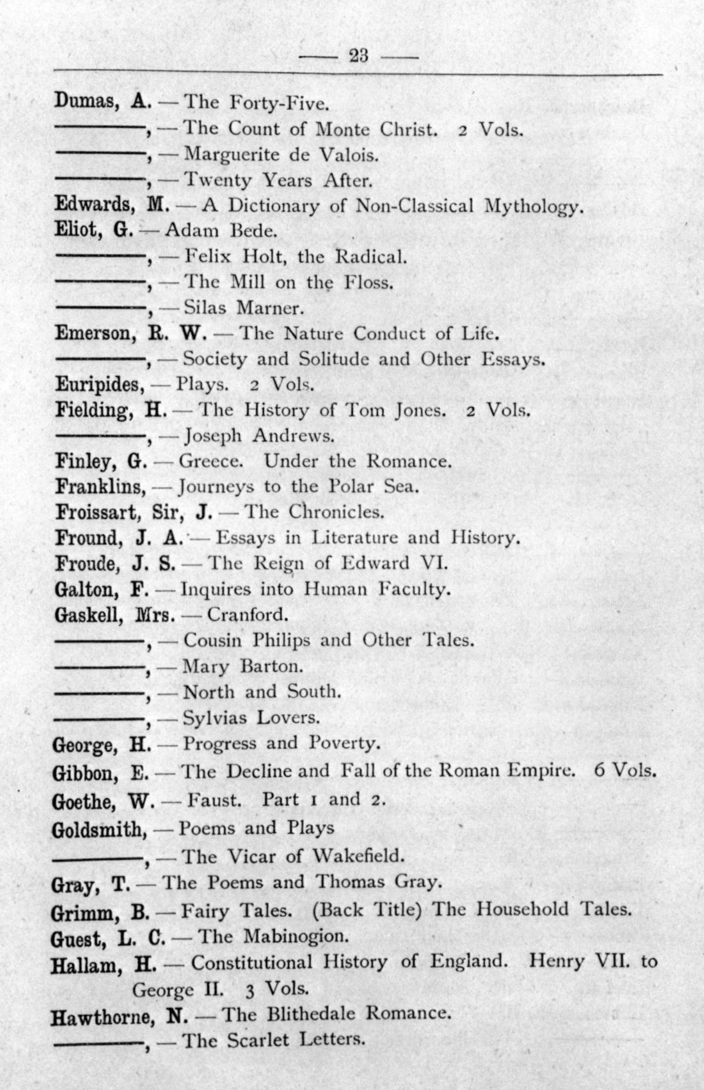

— 23 —

Dumas, A. — The Forty-Five.
————, — The Count of Monte Christ. 2 Vols.
————, — Marguerite de Valois.
————, — Twenty Years After.
Edwards, M. — A Dictionary of Non-Classical Mythology.
Eliot, G. — Adam Bede.
————, — Felix Holt, the Radical.
————, — The Mill on the Floss.
————, — Silas Marner.
Emerson, R. W. — The Nature Conduct of Life.
————, — Society and Solitude and Other Essays.
Euripides, — Plays. 2 Vols.
Fielding, H. — The History of Tom Jones. 2 Vols.
————, — Joseph Andrews.
Finley, G. — Greece. Under the Romance.
Franklins, — Journeys to the Polar Sea.
Froissart, Sir, J. — The Chronicles.
Fround, J. A. — Essays in Literature and History.
Froude, J. S. — The Reign of Edward VI.
Galton, F. — Inquires into Human Faculty.
Gaskell, Mrs. — Cranford.
————, — Cousin Philips and Other Tales.
————, — Mary Barton.
————, — North and South.
————, — Sylvias Lovers.
George, H. — Progress and Poverty.
Gibbon, E. — The Decline and Fall of the Roman Empire. 6 Vols.
Goethe, W. — Faust. Part 1 and 2.
Goldsmith, — Poems and Plays
————, — The Vicar of Wakefield.
Gray, T. — The Poems and Thomas Gray.
Grimm, B. — Fairy Tales. (Back Title) The Household Tales.
Guest, L. C. — The Mabinogion.
Hallam, H. — Constitutional History of England. Henry VII. to George II. 3 Vols.
Hawthorne, N. — The Blithedale Romance.
————, — The Scarlet Letters.

Page twenty-three of the July 1915 number of *Gakuto*, a magazine published by Maruzen Company, Ltd., listing works by Nathaniel Hawthorne and other Western authors. The photograph appears courtesy of Professor David Cody.

> of foreign life to these Japanese girls, and also contain the most idioms. The ordinary readers contain too much description and too [few] everyday matters, and my object at this school is to teach them everyday talk. At the Tokio High School for Girls, which is very successful, I find they are reading Miss Alcott's books as readers, but on examining them I find so much slang in them that I did not care to introduce it at school. What good standard writer has written for children? I don't want too religious Sunday school books, either, as they would be objected to, but then they mustn't be trashy, useless things, and they ought to have a good healthy moral tone to them, too.[3]

Only in the late 1890s and the first decades of the twentieth century did works of literature in English overcome these utilitarian purposes and begin to be appreciated in Japan as literary works of art in and of themselves.

Appendix

In December of 1892, the Bureau of Commerce and Industry in Tokyo published a report entitled *General View of Commerce and Industry in the Empire of Japan.* This was generated in anticipation of Japan's participation in the World's Columbian Exposition of 1893. Among the statistical tables that are provided to demonstrate commercial activity in Japan is one that documents the importation of foreign books into Japan over a five-year period. The only importer listed is Maruzen.

Country	*1887*	*1888*	*1889*	*1890*	*1891*
England	211,770	141,146	93,966	79,059	85,730
France	10,255	10,720	8,926	22,727	10,317
Germany	25,738	24,090	26,136	25,654	27,444
United States	229,559	136,183	104,645	57,896	64,835

These figures suggest several interesting conclusions. It is apparent that books in English were the overwhelming favorite of the Western-

3. This letter is dated 19 June 1887 and was printed in *The Attic Letters: Ume Tsuda's Correspondence to Her American Mother* (New York: Weatherhill, 1991). The volume was edited by Yoshiko Furuki. These quotations appear on pages 290 and 291 of the text.

language materials imported for the Japanese market. We may also assume that the decline in the volume of material from England and the United States is related to the efforts of the Japanese to publish in English themselves. On the other hand, the relatively stable business in books in French and German might imply a steady demand but also that the Japanese made little attempt to print in these languages.

PETER PARLEY'S

UNIVERSAL HISTORY,

ON THE BASIS OF

GEOGRAPHY.

A NEW EDITION, BROUGHT DOWN TO THE PRESENT DAY.

ILLUSTRATED BY 20 MAPS AND 125 ENGRAVINGS.

NEW YORK:
IVISON, PHINNEY, BLAKEMAN & CO.,
CHICAGO: S. C. GRIGGS & CO.

1864.

Title page of *Peter Parley's Universal History* (New York: Ivison, Phinney, Blakeman & Co., 1864).

A Long Incubation before a Renaissance: Hawthorne's Introduction into Meiji Japan

By FUMIO ANO*

IT WAS only after World War II that Nathaniel Hawthorne began to be fully appreciated in Japan. And it was with a new trend in literary interpretation in 1964, the centenary year of his death, that Hawthorne studies truly began to flourish.[1] It will arouse one's interest to know, therefore, that a work by Hawthorne actually exerted a far-reaching influence on Japan in the early days of the Meiji period (1868–1912).

Hawthorne was first introduced into Meiji Japan by Yukichi Fukuzawa (1834–1901), the educator, journalist, and author who greatly contributed to the enlightenment and modernization of Japan. Fukuzawa brought back a copy of Webster's dictionary as "an unequaled treasure in the world" when he first visited the United States in 1860.[2] On his second visit in 1867, Fukuzawa could afford to purchase many more books, including *Peter Parley's Universal History, on the Basis of Geography* (first published in Boston in 1837). As is well known, this book was written by Hawthorne with the help of his sister Elizabeth, and published anonymously as one of the Peter Parley series.[3] However,

*Fumio Ano, a professor of English at Tohoku University, is a founding member of the Nathaniel Hawthorne Society of America and the Nathaniel Hawthorne Society of Japan. See also his "Hawthorne Studies in Japan" and "A Checklist of Theses on Hawthorne in Japan: 1964–1976," which appeared in the 1975 and 1977 issues, respectively, of the *Nathaniel Hawthorne Journal*. The author wishes to thank Kōki Satō, a professor at Shukutoku Junior College, for his "A Hawthorne Checklist in Japan" (*Comparative Literature*, no. 11 for 1968), on which he relied. He also wishes to thank Frederic A. Sharf who suggested that he write on this topic.

1. The *Kenkyusha Yearbook of English* shows that, since 1964, Hawthorne for the most part ranks first among all nineteenth-century American writers who have been the subject of scholarly articles in Japan.
2. "A Memo on the 100th Speech at Mita" ("Mita Enzetsu Dai-Hyakkai no Ki"), *The Complete Works of Yukichi Fukuzawa* (Tokyo: Kokumin Tosho, 1925), 4:577–78.
3. See Hawthorne's letter to his sister Elizabeth, 5 May 1836, in *The Letters, 1813–1843*, vol. 15 of *The Centenary Edition of the Works of Nathaniel Hawthorne*, ed. William Charvat, Roy Harvey Pearce, and Claude M. Simpson (Columbus: Ohio State University Press, 1984), 245.

Frontispiece from *Peter Parley's Universal History* (New York: Ivison, Phinney, Blakeman & Co., 1864). It is entitled "Peter Parley and His Friends at Madrid."

the identity of the author was not known to Fukuzawa, who brought back many copies for students of English to use as a textbook of world history.

The Meiji Restoration was one of the most agitated periods in the history of Japan. To emerge as a modern nation, every aspect of life had to change rapidly and radically, even down to replacing the lunar calendar in 1873 with the Gregorian version used in Europe. To modernize, Japan used the advanced countries of the West as its models; the Meiji period, in particular, was most eager to imitate and assimilate Western culture. Whatever information and knowledge the West gave to Japan was of some use, and even Western ways of thinking, as seen in the works of Shakespeare, were novel—even modern—in those days.[4] To modernize the country, Fukuzawa thought it indispensable to study history, saying that "not reading world history is worse than being mute."[5] For this reason, he made his students at Keio Gijuku, the school he founded in 1858, read *Peter Parley's Universal History,* together with such books as the *Wilson Readers* and Guizot's *The History of Civilization,* translated by William Hazlitt and published in New York in 1859. *The Laws of Keio University (Keio Gijuku Shachū no Yakusoku),* published by the Fukuzawa Memorial Center in 1986, shows that, since Keio's founding, Parley's history had been used as a textbook for many years. On his second visit to the United States in 1867, Fukuzawa also bought books for the Sendai clan to use as textbooks at Yōkendō, a school run by the clan, and among these were twenty-six copies of *Peter Parley's Universal History.*[6] Since it first appeared in 1837, Parley's history was republished in 1860, 1865, 1866, 1868, 1869, 1872, 1873, 1874, and 1886, with major revisions done in 1860, 1874, and 1886. We cannot confirm, however, what edition or editions Fukuzawa obtained in the United States, as no copy remains of the books he brought back in 1867.

Setsurei Miyake (1860–1945) and Nyozekan Hasegawa (1875–1969) were among those who were most impressed by Parley's history. In their memoirs, they look back upon their student days and note that

4. See Yoshinori Yoshitake, "The Introduction of English and American Writers and the Modernization of Japanese Thought" in *Western Writers and Modern Japanese Literature* (Tokyo: Kyōiku Shuppan Center, 1974), 1:7.

5. Yukichi Fukuzawa, "Learning for Getting Enlightened" ("Keimō Tenarai no Bun") in *The Complete Works of Yukichi Fukuzawa,* 2:827.

6. See Kōji Kaneko, "On the List of Foreign Books Kept by Yōkendō," *The Yearbook of Yukichi Fukuzawa,* no. 8 (1981): 207–17.

they read the book with great interest. Nyozekan also admits that he was haunted by a sentence in it: "The people [the Japanese] are idolaters."[7] Naoe Kinoshita (1868–1937) read Parley's history when he was about sixteen, and was greatly influenced by the account of the life of Oliver Cromwell in it. Subsequently, Kinoshita went on to become a social reformer. *Peter Parley's Universal History* had become so popular and influential, especially in the early to middle Meiji period, that, as the 1874 issue of the book explains, "The Japanese seem to wish, too, to know something of the history of the nations from which they have so long lived apart. For every now and then, the publishers of this little book which you are now studying, receive an order from far off Japan for two, four, six hundred copies of Parley's Universal History."[8] The orders from Japan, however, must have diminished soon after, as the book came to be reprinted in Japan in 1881, 1882, 1885, and 1887.

II

In 1871, four years after it was first brought to Japan, selected passages of *Peter Parley's Universal History* were retold in Japanese. Gakujin Neisei, a scholar focusing upon foreign studies, selectively adopted material from the first section of Parley's history, and composed *Western Evening Stories (Seiyō Yobanashi)* in five volumes, "for the purpose of rewarding good and punishing evil."[9] The first three volumes of the translation deal with biblical episodes, such as the Creation, Adam and Eve, the Deluge, and the Tower of Babel, which appear in the chapter on "Asia" in the original; the last two deal with the ancient history of the East. Neisei's book contains eleven illustrations. At least seven of them were taken from the original engravings, but most of them were quite Japanized. Adam and Eve, for example, were drawn just like Prince Izanagi and Princess Izanami, the first god and goddess to appear in Japanese mythology. It is worthy of note that Parley's history played a part in broadening knowledge of the Bible, along with world history,

7. See Takeshi Kimura, *A Study of the History of Literary Exchanges between Japan and America (Nichibei Bungaku Kōryūshi no Kenkyū)* (Tokyo: Kōdansha, 1960), 104–6.

8. *Peter Parley's Universal History* (New York: Ivison, Blakeman, Taylor & Co., 1874), 113. Probably the biggest importer of foreign books including Parley's history in those days was the Maruya-Zenpachi store (founded in 1869), the forerunner of Maruzen Co., Ltd. It is interesting to note the name of "Z. P. Maruya & Co., Tokio" printed on the bottom of the title page of the 1886 issue under the name of Ivison, Blakeman, Taylor & Co.

9. See Gakujin Neisei, introduction to *Western Evening Stories* (Tokyo: Yōgudō, 1871), 1:2.

in a country and an era in which the prohibition against Christianity was only removed in 1873.[10] As John Hyde DeForest (1844–1911), a missionary who participated in founding Tōka School (the forerunner of Tohoku Gakuin University) in Sendai in 1886, wrote in his letter of 18 January of the same year, addressed to his friends at the Yale Divinity School, "Peter Parley never could have had the remotest idea that his simple 'Universal History' would be one of the means of spreading the Jesus Way in this far-off nation with its 'eight hundred thousand gods.'"[11] Neisei also translated books on theology by George W. Knox. According to Masahisa Uemura (1858–1925), a theologian and student of Neisei, his mentor was a man of lax morals who kept a mistress. Neisei, nevertheless, made a contribution to Christianity through his translations.

It was in 1876 that an unabridged version of Parley's history was first translated by Kōhei Makiyama. The Ministry of Education sponsored the publication of this translation, underscoring the enthusiasm the Meiji government had in introducing Western culture. The true identity of the author of Parley's history, however, was not revealed in Japan for many years. This was true in the United States as well. For, as Samuel Griswold Goodrich, planner of the series, admits in his memoirs, Samuel Kettell (1800–55) was mistakenly reported to have been "the veritable Peter Parley."[12] In Japan, many thought that this book had in fact been written by a person named Peter Parley, and a few suspected S. G. Goodrich to be its author, owing to the entry: "Entered, according to the Act of Congress, in the year . . . by S. G. GOODRICH." Neisei, for example, regarded the author to be Peter Parley, and Makiyama explained in his introductory remarks that "the original book was written by Mr. Goodrich under the name of Peter Parley."[13]

It was only in the latter half of the Meiji period that Nathaniel Hawthorne was suspected to have been its author. In the "Editor's File"

10. See Kōki Satō, "S. G. Goodrich and *Peter Parley's Universal History*," *Studies in the History of English Studies* 2 (1970): 17.

11. Charlotte B. DeForest, *The Evolution of a Missionary* (New York: Fleming H. Revell Co., 1914), 137.

12. Samuel Griswold Goodrich, *Recollections of a Lifetime, or Men and Things I Have Seen*, 2 vols. (New York: Miller, Orton & Co., 1856), 2:285.

13. Kōhei Makiyama, trans. *Peter Parley's Universal History (Parley Bankokushi)*, 2 vols. (Tokyo: Ministry of Education, 1876), 1:1.

of the 20 December 1903 issue of the *Student*, for example, a reader asks about the advantages and disadvantages of Parley's and Swinton's histories in terms of style and historicity. The editor replies: "As a history Swinton's book is better than Parley's, but the latter may be better in style, because, in any case, it is an anonymous work of Hawthorne's." Similarly, in *People Today and Yesterday* (*Konjin Kojin*, published in 1906), Kaizan Nakazato (1885–1944) refers to Hawthorne as the author of *The Scarlet Letter* and *Peter Parley's Universal History*. And in "A History of American Literature," a supplement to *A History of English Literature* published in 1907, Wasaburō Asano definitively states that "to tell the truth, *Peter Parley's Universal History*, long favored by Japanese students of English, was written by Hawthorne," in referring to the author's relationship to Goodrich.[14] In a preface to his annotated translation of the book published as late as 1926, however, Tōichi Kita still writes that "there is even an opinion that this book was written by Nathaniel Hawthorne, a great American writer, who wrote books for boys and girls in a refined style."[15] Similarly, in "English Club," a column in the *Rising Generation* of March 1939, Chō Nishimura states that, while its true author must surely be Hawthorne, "the opinion that Peter Parley was the pen name of Goodrich is not without foundation" (80 [1939]). It was not until the November 1959 issue of the same magazine that Saburō Ōta finally settled this problem, explaining all the details of the publication of this book.[16]

Since *Peter Parley's Universal History* was written for children, there is no definite view of history threading through it. Only with the founding of a history department at the University of Tokyo in 1886 did Western-style historical studies begin to develop in Japan. It was then that Western history textbooks began to be written by Japanese scholars. As a matter of course, Parley's history could not help losing its value as a history text. It continued to be read, however, as an English textbook and interesting reading material.[17] Surprisingly, we can still find *The History of America by Peter Parley* in the form of an English textbook recently published by Osaka Kyōiku Tosho Publishing Com-

14. Wasaburō Asano, "A History of American Literature" in *A History of English Literature* (Tokyo: Jinbunsha, 1907), 38.

15. See Satō, "S. G. Goodrich and *Peter Parley's Universal History*," 8.

16. Saburō Ōta, "Hawthorne and *Peter Parley's Universal History*," *Rising Generation* 105 (1959): 406–7.

17. Satō, "S. G. Goodrich and *Peter Parley's Universal History*," 13–16.

pany (containing the section of Parley's history dealing with North America).[18]

III

Early in the Meiji period, Japanese students came to know English and American writers mostly through English textbooks, such as the *New National Reader, Union Reader,* and *Swinton's Reader.* These textbooks are supposed to have been brought into Japan from the beginning of the Meiji period. According to Tetsurō Ikeda, English textbooks used in Meiji Japan can roughly be grouped in three periods.[19] The first period covered 1868 to 1885, when imported textbooks were used.[20] The second one extended from 1885 to 1897, when textbooks reprinted in Japan were available. The third period (after 1897) is that in which mostly Japanese-made textbooks were employed. One of the most widely used textbooks during the Meiji period was Charles J. Barnes's *New National Reader.* Included in the *New National Fifth Reader,* for example, was Hawthorne's "Benjamin West," a selection from *Biographical Stories,* accompanied by slightly inaccurate information:

> Nathaniel Hawthorne, one of our best known American writers, was born at Salem, Mass., in 1804. He was graduated at Bowdoin College in 1825.
>
> There were times in the life of Hawthorne when, on account of poor health, he was compelled to give up literary work. On several of these occasions, he filled various minor positions of public trust.
>
> The readiness of his mind for sudden changes of employment, may be illustrated by the following incident. In 1849, he was a surveyor of customs in Boston [*sic*], and lost his position through a change in the national administration. It is related that on the very day he gave up his business duties, he began the composition of "The Scarlet Letter," one of his masterpieces.
>
> Besides the work already mentioned, the most popular of Haw-

18. It is intriguing that, in the introduction, the annotator should still refer to Peter Parley by the pen name of Goodrich.

19. See *One Hundred Years of English Studies in Japan: The Meiji Period* (Tokyo: Kenkyusha, 1968), 362.

20. Maruzen, for example, imported the *Union Fifth Reader* in 1883, 1885, 1888, and 1890; the *New American Fifth Reader* in 1883; and *Swinton's Fourth Reader* and *Fifth Reader and Speaker* in 1885, 1888, and 1890.

Photograph of Nathaniel Hawthorne taken in London in 1860 by J. J. E. Mayall. This image is known as the Bennoch photograph.

thorne's books are "Twice-told Tales," "The House of the Seven Gables," "The Marble Faun," and of his juvenile works,—"Tanglewood Tales," and "[A] Wonder Book."

Hawthorne died at Plymouth, New Hampshire, in 1864.[21]

Included in *Swinton's Fifth Reader and Speaker,* which was first reprinted in Japan in 1888, were "The Sunken Treasure," an episode from *Grandfather's Chair,* "Oliver Cromwell," a life story from *Biographical Stories,* and "My Oratorical Experience," an extract from *Our Old Home.* It may be observed that all these stories have one thing in common: they have clearly told, universal moral notions on life that were supposed to be useful in educating people. What is more, Hawthorne's works were presumed to be excellent for the study of English, and seem to have been imported frequently for this purpose.[22] Some of Hawthorne's works were also soon reprinted in Japan as English textbooks. Sanseidō Publishing Company, for example, published *Selections from Twice-told Tales* (1895), *A Wonder Book* (1903), *Grandfather's Stories* (1903), *The Golden Touch* (1907), *Biographical Stories* (1908), and *Ten Twice-told Tales* (1912).[23]

IV

While students of English had every now and then come across Hawthorne in English textbooks, it was only in 1880 that the general readership first encountered his name transcribed in kanji, or Chinese characters. Masanao Nakamura (1832–91), a professor of English studies and Chinese classics, translated English social reformer Samuel Smiles's book *Character* (1871) under the title of *Seiyō Hinkōron.* In chapter 9, Hawthorne is introduced as "the shyest of men"; in chapter 11, a passage from *The Marble Faun* is cited as a way of explaining "the union between man and wife."[24] The passage reads: "In matters of affection,

21. *New National Fifth Reader* (Tokyo: Shōbidō, 1901), 69.

22. In 1890, for example, Maruzen imported *Twice-told Tales* (in 2 vols.), *The Snow-Image, The House of the Seven Gables,* and *Transformation: or, The Romance of Monte Beni* (in 2 vols.); in 1900, Maruzen imported *A Wonder Book, Twice-told Tales* (in 2 vols.), *The Snow-Image,* and three-volume sets of Hawthorne's works: vol. 1 included *Twice-told Tales* and *The Snow-Image,* vol. 2 included *The Scarlet Letter* and *The House of the Seven Gables,* and vol. 3 included *Transformation* and *The Blithedale Romance.*

23. See Shigenobu Sadoya, "Hawthorne and the Meiji Period," *Seinan Gakuin Studies in the English Language and Literature* 6 (1966): 97–98.

24. Samuel Smiles, *Character* (1871; reprint, London: John Murray, 1913), 335–36.

there is always an impassable gulf between man and man. They can never quite grasp each other's hands, and therefore man never derives any intimate help, any heart-sustenance, from his brother man, but from woman—his mother, his sister, or his wife."[25] Needless to say, this book is not literary criticism, and Hawthorne is cited only as an example of one type of character. Together with *Self-Help* (a book by Smiles that had been translated by Nakamura under the title *Saikoku Risshiden* in 1871), the translation of *Character* commanded a wide audience and was a powerful presentation of Western morality to the Japanese public. (It deserves special mention that Nakamura became a Christian who inclined toward Unitarianism in his later years, due to the important role Christian writers and scholars played in enlightening Meiji Japan.)

Nine years after Nakamura gave Hawthorne's name to the public, the very first translation of Hawthorne's work appeared. Masatake Ōshima (1859–1938) translated "David Swan: A Fantasy" ("Yume naranu Yume") in *Women's Magazine (Jogaku Zasshi)* in 1889 (nos. 143–44). It was followed by his translation of "Fancy's Show Box: A Morality" ("Kokoro no Ukie") in *Women's Magazine* of the same year (nos. 145–46). Besides these two stories from *Twice-told Tales,* Ōshima translated three more tales in *Women's Magazine* over the next few years. "The Celestial Rail-road" ("Shin Tenro Rekitei") appeared in 1890 (nos. 238–40); "Egotism; or, The Bosom-Serpent" ("Fukuchū no Hebi") in 1891 (nos. 276–77); and "The Minister's Black Veil" ("Kuro Zukin") in 1892 (nos. 311–13). The first two are taken from *Mosses from an Old Manse,* and the last from *Twice-told Tales.* In 1894, Ōshima compiled "David Swan," "Fancy's Show Box," "The Celestial Rail-road," and "Egotism; or, The Bosom-Serpent" under the title of *Arifure Monogatari.*

The first five translations of Hawthorne's tales all appeared in *Women's Magazine.* This publication, which was first issued in July 1885 and discontinued in February 1904, was based on Christian ideals and played an important part in the education of women during the Meiji period. It worked to improve the social status of Japanese women and contributed to the temperance movement and the initiative to abolish licensed prostitution. An appeal for a campaign against licensed prostitution, for example, can be found just after the translation of "The

25. According to *The Marble Faun* as published in *The Centenary Edition of the Works of Nathaniel Hawthorne* (4:285), however, the first sentence reads "between man and man, there is always an insuperable gulf."

Celestial Rail-road" in issue 240. The appeal reads: "Donations are being made one after another for our campaign against licensed prostitution. All of the donations will be printed in aggregate in the next issue. We solicit anybody interested to contribute any amount of money one likes."[26]

Yoshiharu Iwamoto (1863–1943), the founder and editor of *Women's Magazine,* had been baptized in 1883; through the magazine and his founding of Meiji Girls' High School, he tried to put into practice liberal idealism based on Christianity. The publication of *Women's Magazine* was part of a campaign for enlightenment by a Japanese with a keen awareness of his sense of mission.[27] Soon the number of literary articles began to increase, and such writers as Tōkoku Kitamura (1868–94), Ningetsu Ishibashi (1865–1926), Bimyō Yamada (1868–1910), and Tōson Shimazaki (1872–1943) came to write for it. Iwamoto's editorial policy, however, proved too moralistic. Even when he tried to engage in pure literary criticism, he could not part with his moralistic point of view, and Tōkoku and Tōson drifted away from him to publish their own magazine entitled *Literary World (Bungakukai)* in 1893.[28]

Like Iwamoto, Masatake Ōshima was a Christian; in fact, he was a minister as well as an educator and philologist. He entered Sapporo Agricultural School in 1876, where he was greatly influenced by William Smith Clark (1826–86), ex-dean of Amherst College. Dr. Clark, who is well known in Japan for an inspiring speech ("Boys, Be Ambitious!"), devoted himself to teaching botany and propagating Christianity during his eight-month stay in Japan. In 1937, Ōshima published a book about his teacher entitled *Dr. Clark and His Students.* Kanzō Uchimura (1861–1930) entered the Sapporo school soon after and was converted to Christianity, perhaps due to Ōshima's influence. Uchimura wrote later in his English-language book entitled *How I Became a Christian* (1894) that at college they had called him "a missionary monk."[29]

In 1891, when Ōshima translated "Egotism; or, The Bosom-Serpent," a short introduction to Hawthorne appeared in "A History of American Literature," a supplement to *A History of English Literature.* In

26. *Women's Magazine* no. 240 (1890): 408.

27. *One Hundred Years of English Studies in Japan,* 101.

28. *One Hundred Years of English Studies in Japan,* 102.

29. *The Complete Works of Kanzō Uchimura* (Tokyo: Iwanami Shoten, 1982), 3:18.

the preface, Tamotsu Shibue refers to American literature as nothing but a branch of English literature; in Japan, American literature had long been regarded that way. It was only after World War II that American literature acquired an autonomous status. In Shibue's introduction, Hawthorne's year of birth was given as 1807, and, strangely enough, the title of *The Scarlet Letter* was translated as *Kurenai Shokan,* which literally means a "crimson epistle." The title of Hawthorne's masterpiece was translated into Japanese seemingly without any review of the contents. Shibue was somewhat like Henry James who, as a child, "had a vague belief . . . that the 'letter' in question was one of the documents that come by the post."[30] (Incidentally, Shibue gives one line of introduction to James, referring to *The American* and *The Portrait of a Lady.* His year of birth was also incorrectly cited.) James's critical biography of Hawthorne (1879) had already been imported by Maruzen as early as 1883, but it is not likely that Shibue had read this volume when he wrote "A History of American Literature." In any case, it is peculiar that such a careless introduction should be written when some of Hawthorne's tales were widely disseminated through English textbooks. The introduction does contain one thing of value, however; Shibue acknowledges that Hawthorne was acquainted with the dynamics of psychology, clear examples of which may be found in his works.

One year after Shibue's history of American literature appeared, Shōyō Tsubouchi (1859–1935) published an article, "Two Influences in the Novel" ("Shōsetsu niokeru Ni-Seiryoku"), in the October 1892 issue of *Waseda Literature (Waseda Bungaku),* a magazine he had founded the previous year as a bulletin for the department of literature of Waseda University. Tsubouchi, known as the first translator of the complete works of William Shakespeare, had radically improved the traditional view of fiction. In this article, Tsubouchi perceived the psychologist in Hawthorne and thought that "the chief concern of Hawthorne is not the outward appearance, but the interior recesses," and that "his most psychological novel is *The Marble Faun.*"[31] Whether or not *The Marble Faun* is the most psychological novel may occasion some discussion, but the assertion surely reflects a more modern view of Hawthorne. It is only natural that the psychological aspect of Hawthorne should greatly

30. Henry James, *Hawthorne* (1879; reprint, New York: Great Seal Books, 1956), 87.

31. Shōyō Tsubouchi, "Two Influences in the Novel," *Waseda Literature* (October 1892): 7–8.

interest Tsubouchi who, in *The Essence of the Novel (Shōsetsu Shinzui,* 1885–86), asserted "the novelist should be just like a psychologist," and that "characters in the novel should be created on the basis of the principles of psychology."[32] (In an introductory note to his article, Tsubouchi admits that this is an abridged translation of an article in *Forum,* but it proved difficult to trace the source mentioned here.) "Two Influences in the Novel" was published again in *Literature for Every Occasion (Bungaku Sono Oriori)* in 1896.

In 1893, Tsubouchi translated "Fancy's Show Box" ("Sōzōshi no Kugutsubako") in *Waseda Literature* (nos. 49 and 51), and it is from this tale that he obtained the inspiration for *A Dream of a Millionaire (Aru Fugō no Yume),* a one-act play he wrote in 1920. In the same year, he also dramatized "Dr. Heidegger's Experiment," a story in *Twice-told Tales.* This was to become a one-act play entitled *Kaishunsen no Shiken,* which literally means "an experiment concerning the return of spring."[33] The whimsical element of "Fancy's Show Box" and the intriguing plot of "Dr. Heidegger's Experiment" must surely have appealed to Tsubouchi.

One more introduction of Hawthorne appeared in a biographical dictionary published in 1892. Bimyō Yamada, a novelist who belonged to the Friends of the Inkstone (Ken'yūsha), edited *An International Biographical Dictionary (Bankoku Jinmei Jiten)* in two volumes. The first volume included a short, inadequate biography of Hawthorne in which only *Twice-told Tales* and *The Scarlet Letter* were mentioned.

In 1892, four more tales were translated, in addition to "The Minister's Black Veil." Shōyō Matsui (1870–1933) published a serialized translation of "The Great Stone Face" ("Kyojin Seki"), a tale from *The Snow-Image,* in supplements to the *Yomiuri* newspaper (nos. 5232, 5237, 5239, 5243, 5258, and 5262). Matsui was a student of Shōyō Tsubouchi, and is known today mainly for his translations of European dramas. Although translated only once during the Meiji period, "The Great Stone Face" has long been a favorite of Japanese readers. The morality depicted in it—particularly the modesty of the protagonist and his never-ending pursuit of an ideal—has always appealed to Japanese sensibilities.

32. Shōyō Tsubouchi, *The Essence of the Novel* (1885–86; reprint, Tokyo: Chikuma Shobō, 1956), 92.

33. See Yoshinori Yoshitake, *A History of Translation in the Meiji and Taisho Periods* (Tokyo: Kenkyusha, 1959), 135–36.

Directly after, Koshoshi Miyazaki (1864–1922) translated "The Village Uncle" ("Gyoō"), a tale in *Twice-told Tales,* for the newspaper *Kokumin* in 1892 (nos. 663–66 and 673–74); he translated "The Gray Champion" ("Shirahige Musha"), another story from *Twice-told Tales,* in the same paper (nos. 652–57). The greatest achievement of Miyazaki, however, was not his translations of Hawthorne, but his study of William Wordsworth. He published in 1893 the first well-organized critical biography of the poet to appear in Japan. Although Miyazaki was deeply affected by Wordsworth, it is still possible to trace Hawthorne's influence on his two novels, *White Clouds* (*Hakuun,* 1887) and *Confession* (*Jihaku,* 1908).[34] It is important to note that Miyazaki was a Protestant minister as well as a poet and novelist. He had been baptized in 1886 and devoted himself to the propagation of Christianity, although he ultimately became a fanatical nationalist in his later years. In the words of Rintarō Fukuhara, "English literature in Japan, especially that of the Meiji period, should be considered in terms of Christianity."[35] It should be remembered that even a book of world history was utilized in broadening knowledge of the Bible.

In 1886, Shiken Morita (1861–97), primarily known as a translator of Victor Hugo, translated "The Intelligence Office" ("Yōtatsu Kaisha"), a tale from *Mosses from an Old Manse,* in *A Companion to the People (Kokumin no Tomo),* nos. 171–72 and 174. This was a magazine first published in 1887 and edited by Sohō Tokutomi (1863–1957). Together with *Women's Magazine, A Companion to the People* was among the representative publications that made a great contribution to the popularization of literature in the inchoate stage of its development in Japan. Morita's translation of "The Intelligence Office" was republished in *The Third National Novel (Daisan Kokumin Shōsetsu)* in 1893.

Two additional translations of Hawthorne's tales appeared in 1893. Besides Shōyō Tsubouchi's translation of "Fancy's Show Box," Morita translated "David Swan" ("Hirune") in *An Anthology of Modern Masterpieces (Kinsei Meika Bunshū)* for the second time. Although he contributed greatly to the translation of foreign literature, Morita's "David Swan" was criticized by Ōson Sakurai for errors and frequent omissions.[36]

34. See Kōki Satō, "Hawthorne," *Western Writers and Modern Japanese Literature* (Tokyo: Kyōiku Shuppan Center, 1974), 1:190.

35. Rintarō Fukuhara, *English in Japan* (Tokyo: Kenkyusha, 1958), 36–37.

36. See Sadoya, "Hawthorne and the Meiji Period," 101.

Of all the contents of *Twice-told Tales,* "David Swan" was the most frequently translated during the Meiji period; there were versions in 1889, 1893, 1894, 1902, 1906, and 1909. This tale has remained the most popular, and I, myself, remember reading it in an English textbook and being obliged to repeat from memory the initial part when I was a high school student in 1949: "We can be but partially acquainted even with events which actually influence our course through life, and our final destiny." The well-balanced composition, the beautiful styling of the tale, and, above all, the easily understood moral have long appealed to Japanese readers. The next most frequently presented tale was "Fancy's Show Box," which was translated four times during the Meiji period: in 1889, 1893, 1894, and 1906. The allegorical approach of the tale must have attracted Meiji readers. Moreover, it is likely that the explicit subtitle, "A Morality," attracted attention above all else.

In 1894, an anonymous translation of "Mr. Higginbotham's Catastrophe" ("Higginbotham no Sainan: Godo Bikkuri"), a story from *Twice-told Tales,* was printed alongside the original text in the *New Magazine* (nos. 44–50). Shozan Nishimura translated it again as "Mura no Daijiken" in 1905 in *Literary Club (Bungei Kurabu),* vol. 1, no. 5. It has been a common practice since the Meiji period in English magazines to print the texts of English and American literature along with notes and translations for students of English to study by themselves. The *New Magazine,* first issued in 1894, was an example of one such publication dedicated to the pursuit of English language and literature. Other examples included the *Student* (first issued in 1885), the *Museum* (first issued in 1890), the *Far East* (first issued in 1896), the *English World* (first issued in 1897), and the *Rising Generation* (first issued in 1898), which is still being published monthly. It is worth notice that in 1894 Takeki Ōwada (1857–1910), the poet and literary critic, published *Lives of English and American Men of Letters (Eibei Bunjin Den),* which included a longer and much more satisfactory Hawthorne biography than Shibue's. In this book, Ōwada introduced thirty-five English and American literary figures. The six American writers he selected were Washington Irving, William Cullen Bryant, Ralph Waldo Emerson, Henry Wadsworth Longfellow, John Greenleaf Whittier, and Hawthorne. The biography contains one mistake, however. In giving an account of Hawthorne's death, Ōwada writes: "Hawthorne set sail for the other world from the port of Plymouth," meaning that the author believed Hawthorne died in Plymouth, Massachusetts, rather than his true place of death, Plymouth, New Hampshire.[37]

In *Imperial Literature (Teikoku Bungaku)* for 1895, Rinryō Kōsai wrote an article on "Chikamatsu Sōrinshi's View of Life" ("Chikamatsu Sōrinshi ga Jinseikan"), vol. 1, no. 2. In it, he compared Monzaemon Chikamatsu with Hawthorne and William Makepeace Thackeray, judging the latter two as grave and serious writers.

V

In 1895, the Sino-Japanese War ended in a victory for Japan, greatly influencing the growth and development of the country in many ways. With the victory, Meiji Japan awakened to its national identity and gained self-confidence. One by-product was a desire for Japan's own unique literature. The first issue of *Imperial Literature* was published in just such a climate in January of 1895, and its preface strongly advocated the need for a national literature. Nationalism before the Sino-Japanese War was anti-Western in some respects, but after the war it became quite different; in order to create its own literature, one which could be touted throughout the modern world, Japan tried to consume and assimilate Western culture even more avariciously. Consequently, foreign writers were introduced with greater frequency.

In the same year, Masatake Shinoda translated five stories from *Biographical Stories* under the title of *Eibei Goketsu Denki Monogatari*, which may be translated as *Lives of Five Great Men of England and America.* Hawthorne's work includes six lives, the sixth being Queen Christina's, but Shinoda's translation excludes her biography. As he admitted in his preface, Shinoda's aim in translating these stories was to educate morally both children and adults. Stories of great Western men were supposed to be quite useful in educating and enlightening people in Meiji Japan. As previously mentioned, Naoe Kinoshita actually decided to become a social reformer, having been influenced by the life of Cromwell that he had read in *Peter Parley's Universal History*. Kiyoshi Yoshida translated *Biographical Stories (Denki Monogatari)* again in 1906, and this time the life of Queen Christina was included in the translation.

From 1896 to 1902, the only writings concerning Hawthorne were Shōyō Tsubouchi's "Two Influences in the Novel," reprinted in *Literature*

37. Takeki Ōwada, *Lives of English and American Men of Letters* (Tokyo: Hakubunkan, 1894), 171.

for Every Occasion in 1896, and Zein Kohinata's translation of "David Swan" published in *Imperial Literature* in 1902 (vol. 8, no. 8). In 1903, translations of three tales were published: "The Golden Touch," a story in *A Wonder Book,* translated as "Ōgon Ō" by Shikei Fujii, in *Imperial Literature* (vol. 9, no. 4); "The Sister Years," a story in *Twice-told Tales,* translated as "Joya Monogatari" by Sekiō Rakuraku in *Myōjō,* a magazine founded by Tekkan Yosano in 1899 (no. 2); and "Endicott and the Red Cross," another story from *Twice-told Tales,* translated as "Kokki Bundan" by Hōmei Iwano (1873–1920) in *Myōjō* (no. 8).

What deserves special mention is that it was not until 1903 that the first translation of one of Hawthorne's novels appeared. Tokuma Tominaga (1875–1930) translated *The Scarlet Letter* under the title of *Hi Monji.* He was a missionary of the Christian church of Japan, and emphasized the Puritan blood in Hawthorne's veins in a preface to his translation. Kiyoshi Satō, the second translator of the novel (1917), and Yoshirō Jin, the third translator (1923), also emphasized Puritanism in their interpretations of the novel. In a preface to his translation, Satō refers to Hawthorne as "the John Bunyan of the nineteenth century."[38] "The Custom-House," the introduction to *The Scarlet Letter,* was not included in Tominaga's translation, and has not been included in many of the translations since then except in Kochō Baba's (1927). This unique introduction has long been neglected as being rather unimportant.

Of all Hawthorne's novels, *The Scarlet Letter* has been the most popular with the public as well as being deemed the most important to Hawthorne scholars in Japan. More than ten translations of the novel have appeared since Tominaga first did it in 1903. On the other hand, it was only in 1964, the centenary year of Hawthorne's death, that *The House of the Seven Gables* was first translated. *The Marble Faun* and *The Blithedale Romance* were translated in 1984, and *Fanshawe* in 1990.

In 1904, Shinobu Matsumoto translated "Dr. Heidegger's Experiment" ("Kushiki Jikken") in the *Flower of the Heart (Kokoro no Hana),* vol. 8, nos. 3–4. This magazine was first issued in 1898 as a bulletin for lovers of tanka, the thirty-one-syllable Japanese poetic form. Later, Matsumoto included this tale in his translation of *Twice-told Tales* after polishing it. Shiken Saitō translated it again as "Furōsen" in 1905 in *Literary World (Bungei Kai),* vol. 4, no. 4. Saitō's, however, was

38. See Satō, "Hawthorne," 191.

an adaptation rather than a translation: all the characters are given Japanese names, and his own descriptions are added freely. The curious theme of the elixir of life in this tale, in any case, must have intrigued these two translators. In the same year, an anonymous introduction to Hawthorne appeared in the "Miscellanea" section of *Imperial Literature* (vol. 10, no. 12). In it, the dark side of Hawthorne is emphasized, and he is regarded as "a nineteenth-century Hamlet" who is just like "a living ghost," whose life is that of "an owl," and whose gloominess is purported to be such as to freeze the heart.[39] It is true that Hawthorne was frequently considered too gloomy to Japanese readers during the Meiji period.

In 1905, Shozan Nishimura wrote a more detailed life of Hawthorne in his "Thirty-Six Great Men of Letters of the World" ("Sekai Sanjū-roku Bungō") contained in the *World of Middle School (Chūgaku Sekai),* vol. 8, no. 12. His introduction to Hawthorne gives a fairly good account of this writer. It is interesting to note that his novels are compared with Shakespeare's *Hamlet.* Nishimura regarded Hawthorne as a lonely, moralistic critic of nineteenth-century America, concluding:

> Nineteenth-century America, after all, was nothing but one act of an opera which is obsequious to the God of Pleasure. All men drank and sang, and all women danced with their skirts waving about them. In this state of things, however, Nathaniel Hawthorne alone dared to criticize all aspects of the nineteenth century severely. Oh, he was one of the critics of the age![40]

Nishimura's article also contained some illustrations. One of them is Hawthorne's portrait, probably from the steel engraving by Thomas Phillibrown that was used as a frontispiece to *Twice-told Tales* (Boston: Ticknor, Reed, and Fields, 1851); the two others were a picture of the Old Manse and a portrait of Sophia, which may be from the etching by S. A. Schoff. That same year, two other portraits of Hawthorne appeared in print in Japan: one was in an extra summer issue of the *World of Middle School* (vol. 8, no. 8), and the other was in *New Voice (Shinsei),* vol. 13, no. 1. The former is probably the photograph by

39. *Imperial Literature* 10 (1904): 1733.

40. Shozan Nishimura, "Thirty-Six Great Men of Letters of the World," *World of Middle School* 8 (1905): 153.

Carte-de-visite of Sophia Hawthorne taken in 1861 by Silsbee, Case, & Co., a Boston photographic studio. The photograph was donated to the Peabody Essex Museum by Barbara L. Bacheler.

Alexander Gardner (1862), and the latter may be the line engraving by Oliver Pelton (1873).[41]

In *People Yesterday and Today* published in 1906, Kaizan Nakazato refers to Hawthorne as "an inborn complainer . . . who loves solitude."[42] In the same year, Shiken Saitō translated "The Ambitious Guest" ("Ichiya Domari"), a tale from *Twice-told Tales,* and included it in *A Collection of Old and New Writings (Shinko Bunrin),* vol. 2, no. 3. This tale has been a favorite of Japanese readers since the Meiji period. The theme of futility in the destiny of man surely sounded a resonant chord with the Japanese sensibility. The same story appeared again as "Taibō o Idakeru Kyakujin" in Shinobu Matsumoto's translation of *Twice-told Tales* published the same year; it was then released again as "Hazama no Yado" in Kyūshiro Honma's *New Translations of Masterpieces (Meicho Shin-Yaku)* in 1907.

Matsumoto also produced a collection of fifteen stories from *Twice-told Tales* in 1906. The fifteen included "Dr. Heidegger's Experiment," "The Vision of the Fountain," "The Minister's Black Veil," "Fancy's Show Box," "David Swan," "The Ambitious Guest," "The Sister Years," "Endicott and the Red Cross," "Howe's Masquerade," "Lady Eleanore's Mantle," "Old Esther Dudley," "A Rill from the Town Pump," "The Wedding Knell," "Peter Goldthwaite's Treasure," and "The Seven Vagabonds." In a preface to the translation, Matsumoto stated that out of the thirty-nine existing stories, these fifteen would be enough to understand the entirety of *Twice-told Tales.* On the first page of Matsumoto's book was printed a portrait of Hawthorne in his later years. This may be from the engraving by John Andrew that was used as a frontispiece to Rose Hawthorne Lathrop's *Memories of Hawthorne* (1897). His book also contained a short biography of Hawthorne, based on that of William P. Trent's *A History of American Literature.* Most Meiji-period critics apparently believed that *Twice-told Tales* was the best of all Hawthorne's works. One exception was Lafcadio Hearn (1850–1904) who became a naturalized Japanese citizen, assuming the name of Yakumo Koizumi in 1896. In the course of his seven years' service at the University of Tokyo (1896–1903), Hearn gave a lecture entitled "Notes on American Literature" in the fall of 1898, in which he said

41. In order to confirm the artists, I relied on Rita K. Gollin, *Portraits of Nathaniel Hawthorne: An Iconography* (DeKalb, Ill.: Northern Illinois University Press, 1983).

42. Kaizan Nakazato, *People Yesterday and Today* (Tokyo: Ryūbunkan, 1906), 39.

Carte-de-visite of (from left to right) James Fields, Nathaniel Hawthorne, and William Ticknor, photographed by James Wallace Black in 1861 or 1862.

that "the stories that he [Hawthorne] wrote during his early struggles were not his best; they are called the 'Twice-told Tales.'"[43] He also commented that "The 'Twice-told Tales' are of [*sic*] partly historical, and mostly dull."[44] Hearn praised *Mosses from an Old Manse,* and referred to "Rappaccini's Daughter" as "the most excellent that Hawthorne ever wrote."[45] In this respect, Hearn's opinion was exceptional for the Meiji period. From the beginning, he was rather critical of Hawthorne. Preferring Poe, he harshly declared, "A great deal of the material published in the definitive edition of Hawthorne's works is little more than rubbish."[46]

In all, one novel and a total of forty-nine tales by Hawthorne were translated during the Meiji period. Thirty-six of the tales (approximately seventy-three percent) were from *Twice-told Tales,* while five were from *Mosses from an Old Manse,* five from *Biographical Stories,* one from *The Snow-Image,* and one from *A Wonder Book.* It was only following World War II that Hawthorne was reevaluated as a writer who wrote very modern, complex works. Such tales as "Young Goodman Brown," "My Kinsman, Major Molineux," "Roger Malvin's Burial," "The Birth-mark," and "The Artist of the Beautiful," all included in *Mosses from an Old Manse,* were not translated until after the centenary year of Hawthorne's death.

In 1907, Yoshijirō Fukazawa published an annotated and serialized interlinear translation of "The Hollow of the Three Hills" ("Kami Oroshi") in the *Rising Generation* (vol. 18, nos. 1–6). In the same year, Kyūshirō Honma translated "The Vision of the Fountain" ("Izumi no Gen'ei") in *New Translations of Masterpieces,* along with "The Ambitious Guest," and Wasaburō Asano published a more substantial introduction and interpretation of Hawthorne in "A History of American Literature," a supplement to *A History of English Literature.* In this latter work, Asano regards Hawthorne and Poe as writers who "really displayed originality and explored an untrodden wilderness, though their styles and dispositions were greatly different."[47] Asano drew upon James's

43. Lafcadio Hearn, *A History of English Literature in a Series of Lectures* (Tokyo: Hokuseidō Press, 1930), 951.

44. Hearn, *A History of English Literature,* 958.

45. Hearn, *A History of English Literature,* 958.

46. Hearn, *A History of English Literature,* 949.

47. Asano, "A History of American Literature," 36.

biography of Hawthorne as a reference and, just as James did, pointed out that "most of the characters depicted by Hawthorne are figures representing spiritual activities," asserting that, "Such figures live not in the actual world, but in the inner recesses of the human heart."[48] Asano also attached importance to "new morals" in many of Hawthorne's tales, thinking that "to read Hawthorne's tales is to look into situations of life."[49] It may be worthy of notice that Asano referred to "Young Goodman Brown" as an important work, along with "Rappaccini's Daughter."

In his interpretation of *The Scarlet Letter,* Asano compared Hawthorne with Maupassant, remarking, "if Maupassant chose such a subject, he would do his best to depict adultery itself."[50] A deep interest in French naturalism had led to the introduction of Maupassant into Japan, and critics often discussed Hawthorne in relation to this French novelist. Tengen Inoue (1884–1928), the editor of *Waseda Literature,* mentioned Hawthorne in his discussion on Maupassant in "Literary Reviews and Criticisms of Life" ("Bungei Hihyō to Jinsei Hihyō"):

> Maupassant is the best of all popular novelists. His works have the excitement of life which gives us direct images of actual life more than the deep recesses of the inner life depicted by Hawthorne.[51]

In "Maupassant and Modern English Short-Story Writers" ("Maupassant to Eikoku Gendai no Tanpen-Sakka"), issued in the *World of Writing (Bunsho Sekai),* vol. 7, no. 4, Kameo Chiba introduced Arthur Conan Doyle's opinion that Julian Hawthorne's short stories were more attractive than his father's.

An article about *The Scarlet Letter* appeared in 1908 in the *Shirogane Bulletin (Shirogane Gakuhō),* a publication of Meiji Gakuin University. In "Reading *The Scarlet Letter*" ("*The Scarlet Letter* o Yomu"), Shirō Segawa expressed the idea that Hawthorne was "one of the believers in Puritanism." He praised Hawthorne for omitting the details of Hester's adultery with Dimmesdale, yet criticized the author for displaying too

48. Asano, "A History of American Literature," 41.
49. Asano, "A History of American Literature," 42.
50. Asano, "A History of American Literature," 43.
51. Tengen Inoue, "Literary Reviews and Criticisms of Life," *Waseda Literature* (April 1909): 4.

Photograph of the Boston publisher James T. Fields.

much "fancy" and "imagination."[52] These were the chief defects of the novel in Segawa's opinion. It should not come as a surprise that Segawa identified the omission of the description of adultery as an estimable decision. Segawa was a student of the department of divinity at Meiji Gakuin University when he wrote this article. After graduation, he studied theology in the United States, and began teaching theology at his alma mater as an assistant professor in 1915.

In 1909, Hōmei Iwano translated "David Swan" ("Sugiyuku Kafuku") in *Modern English Literature (Kinsei Eibungaku)*. Iwano's was the sixth and last translation of the tale during the Meiji period. In the same year, *An Encyclopedia of Literature (Bungei Hyakka Zensho)* was edited by Hōgetsu Shimamura (1871–1918), critic, playwright, and a student of Shōyō Tsubouchi's. Shimamura's encyclopedia includes a history of American literature in which many important issues concerning Hawthorne were mentioned: for example, Hawthorne was again described as "the most thoroughgoing interpreter of New England Puritanism"; his works were alleged to have always two opposite sides, one dark, the other light; *The Scarlet Letter* and *The Marble Faun* were viewed as dealing with the horrible power of sin and the influences it exerts upon the psychology of man; and the actual and the imaginary were seen as being intertwined in all of Hawthorne's works.[53]

In Shimamura's encyclopedia, the plot of *The Scarlet Letter* was summarized in the column, "Explanatory Notes of Masterpieces," and the life of Hawthorne was presented in the category of "Biographies of Writers." It is humorous to find in the explanatory note of *The Scarlet Letter* that the native American is still introduced as an "indojin," suggesting the connection to India or the East Indies. (Hawthorne's portrait printed on page 532 of this 1909 edition may be the carte-de-visite issued by J. J. E. Mayall.)

We should not forget that in 1910 one of Hawthorne's letters was translated by Hiroshi Ishikawa in *Letters by Eminent Men of the West (Taisei Meika no Tegami)*. The letter was entitled "Unnecessary Life Insurance" ("Fuhitsuyōnaru Seimei-Hoken") and was, in fact, the first two-thirds of a letter Hawthorne wrote to Elizabeth Peabody on 25 May 1851. In it, he politely declines the life insurance suggested by Elizabeth. The translator seems to have taken an interest in the polite manner of refusal

52. Shirō Segawa, "Reading *The Scarlet Letter*," *Shirogane Bulletin*, no. 14 (1908): 13.

53. Hōgetsu Shimamura, ed., *An Encyclopedia of Literature* (Tokyo: Ryūbunkan, 1909), 531–32.

intended not to displease others. He must also have felt that this would serve as a good model for letter writing. It is interesting that Hawthorne's letter should be presented as an example of consideration for others or a lesson in social etiquette.

VI

This has largely been a chronological treatment of the introduction of Hawthorne into Japan. Hawthorne certainly influenced many important Japanese writers, including Naoe Kinoshita, Shōyō Tsubouchi, and Koshoshi Miyazaki. It is not reasonable to suppose that we can identify his literary influence on other Meiji writers as well, but it is indisputable that Hawthorne exerted a considerable influence upon Sōseki Natsume (1867–1916), one of the greatest writers of the Meiji period. Natsume was well acquainted with Hawthorne's work: in *And Then* (*Sorekara,* 1909), for example, the name of Hawthorne is mentioned in a chat between Takagi and Daisuke, the protagonist of the novel. From consulting the Sōseki Collection, we can confirm that Natsume read at least one of Hawthorne's novels.[54] According to his note on the back leaf of the book, Natsume obtained a copy of *The House of the Seven Gables* (London: George Bell & Sons, 1888) at Nakanishiya Bookstore, Kanda, Tokyo, on 31 March 1889. He read it carefully, leaving notes in the margins, most of which are English explanations for words such as "propinquity," "Daguerreotype," "anomaly," and "contumaciously." Although the library does not include *The Scarlet Letter,* it is quite possible that Natsume read it, and that he read other works of Hawthorne as well.

Like Hawthorne, Natsume deals with adultery in the trilogy of *Sanshirō* (1908), *And Then,* and *The Gate* (*Mon,* 1910). These works deal with guilt in terms of isolation and the problem of "the unconscious hypocrite." Adhering to the concepts of Western social customs, monogamy was emphasized, and adultery was regarded as a grave crime in Meiji Japan. Punishment for adultery was formally enacted in 1882, and only abolished in 1947. Although the rules were slightly relaxed in 1908, one year before Natsume published *And Then,* the regulations were still rigorous, especially for women. Just as Hawthorne showed Hester and Dimmesdale forced to live in the fetters of seventeenth-century Puritan society, Natsume presented Daisuke and his partner, Michiyo, as having

54. The 3,068 books owned by Natsume are now kept in the Tohoku University Library, and these are known as the Sōseki Collection.

to live in the still feudalistic, Confucian atmosphere of an only superficially modernized society. Hawthorne depicted problematical dimensions of Puritanism in *The Scarlet Letter,* while Natsume conveyed the disparities of the Japanese law in *And Then.*

We can certainly find other close resemblances in description between *And Then* and *The Scarlet Letter.* Attention, first of all, should be paid to Daisuke's symbolic hand gestures, reminiscent of similar usage in *The Scarlet Letter.* It can also be conjectured that the last scene of *And Then* was inspired by chapter 17 ("The Flight of Two Owls") from *The House of the Seven Gables,* in which Clifford and Hepzibah run away out of the house and board a train aimlessly. Almost in imitation of Clifford, Daisuke boards a train with no destination in mind. Although these are merely a few details that attest to a familiarity with Hawthorne on the part of Natsume, it would be comparatively easy to demonstrate the considerable influence exerted upon him by Hawthorne.

Hawthorne studies have clearly been advancing and flourishing in Japan in recent years. One could even maintain that there is a Hawthorne renaissance underway. His introduction into Meiji Japan must be viewed as a critical part of this evolutionary development. We must remember that, while he is being scrutinized by Japanese academics in a modern critical fashion today, Hawthorne as an author was brought into the country almost solely as a vehicle for the adoption of English. This intimate association between Hawthorne texts and the learning of the English language in Meiji Japan created an extraordinary incubation period. This historic linkage would not have yielded much, however, without the seemingly inveterate interest in Hawthorne that Japanese readers and scholars continue to demonstrate.

Photograph of Nathaniel Hawthorne taken in London in 1860 by J. J. E. Mayall. This image is known as the Holden pose.

Hawthorne in Japan: Some Recent Studies, 1975–1991

By DAVID CODY*

Although the life and works of Nathaniel Hawthorne have long been studied by Japanese literary scholars, American scholars interested in Hawthorne in nineteenth-century American literature in general, or in the development of American studies in Japan have found it exceedingly difficult to gain access to Japanese literary criticism. The intent of the present article is thus to provide American Hawthornians with a glimpse of some recent trends and developments in Hawthorne studies in Japan. To this end, I have summarized a number of scholarly essays that have appeared in Japanese literary journals in the past fifteen years or so—a period during which such studies reached a new level of sophistication and maturity.

Only works written in English (or for which English summaries are available) have been considered here, none of the articles and essays considered was published before 1975, and all were published in Japan rather than in the United States or elsewhere. The year 1975 was chosen as a convenient *point d'appui* because Professor Fumio Ano's bibliographical essay, "Hawthorne Studies in Japan," which appeared in the *Nathaniel Hawthorne Journal* in that year, takes into consideration works on Hawthorne published after 1964 (the Hawthorne centenary year, which was also, as Ano remarks, "the beginning of an epoch in Hawthorne studies in Japan").[1]

Most American scholars remain unfamiliar with Japanese scholarship relating to Hawthorne and his works (even that which has been written in English) because the scholarly journals in which they have

*David Cody is a professor of English at Hartwick College in Oneonta, New York, and was a Fulbright specialist lecturer in American literature at Hokkaido University in Japan. His special interest in Hawthorne is obviously shared by many of his Japanese contemporaries, as the following article will reveal.

1. Fumio Ano, "Hawthorne Studies in Japan," *Nathaniel Hawthorne Journal* (1975): 265.

appeared do not circulate widely in this country. A number (but by no means all) of the essays mentioned here found a place in one of the annual bibliographies published by the Modern Language Association, and a few have been cited in the chapters on "Japanese contributions" to the study of American literature (edited, in alternating years, by Keiko Beppu and Hiroko Sato), which have appeared annually in *American Literary Scholarship*, but although they have—in theory at least—been accessible to those American scholars who might choose to seek them out, in practice most have been impossible to locate. Some few may be available through the American interlibrary loan system, but most are to be found only within Japan itself, and I received copies of many of these only because Fumio Ano of Tohoku University and Atsushi Katayama of Hokkaido University were generous enough to obtain them for me, at considerable expense to themselves in terms of time and trouble.[2] It was also through their efforts that I was able to obtain copies of a number of articles and essays that had not, in fact, found their way into the MLA bibliographies, works whose existence would not otherwise have come to my attention. As I have already noted, however, the essays summarized here represent only a sampling—although it is, hopefully, a representative one—of the Hawthorne scholarship produced in Japan in recent years. I trust that I have not done violence to the views expressed by any of the authors whose works I have considered here, or distorted them more than condensation and occasional differences in language have made unavoidable. I have done my best to avoid interpolating my own opinions on Hawthorne's work, or my own views as to the validity of the premise upon which a particular essay is based, and in this sense my function has been that of a compiler rather than a critic.

The history of Hawthorne scholarship in Japan is a complex one, for it is also the history of an encounter between the scholars of one culture and the works of an author who belonged not merely to a different culture, but to a different century and a different world. The history in question has thus been part of the larger and even more complex process by means of which Japanese scholars have sought to arrive at an understanding of American culture through the analysis of the works

2. I would also like to express my gratitude to Ms. Christina Yu, a reference librarian at the Z. Smith Reynolds Library at Wake Forest University, who searched high and low for the necessary articles.

of one of its artists. This process, which had its origin in the encounter between Japanese culture and the Western world, found its first great impetus during the Meiji era, which began in 1868—four years after Hawthorne's death—and lasted until 1912. During the period following the Meiji Restoration, and particularly after the emperor's Charter Oath of 1868 committed the government to the pursuit of knowledge and wisdom throughout the world, Japanese society underwent tremendous changes: the principle of constitutionalism was adopted, feudalism was abolished, the idea of universal education on the Western model was accepted, and the nation as a whole was made much more open to certain Western influences (including literature, to some degree) in order that it might eventually achieve military, industrial, and material equality with the Western powers. The small part of this historical process that deals with the introduction of Hawthorne into Japan has been much commented upon, although not explored in its entirety, by various scholars, and in the brief summary that follows I am largely indebted to their efforts.[3]

At some point during the early years of the Meiji era, a few of Hawthorne's tales began to appear in the English-language textbooks and the "cram-books" used by senior high school students when studying for their examinations in English—and some of his stories and sketches are, in fact, still used for the same purpose today. In 1966, Shinichiro Noriguchi's rationale for writing an essay on Hawthorne's use of archetypal symbolism was that an explanation of Hawthorne's use of such symbolism would benefit the many students at the secondary school level who were required to study *The Scarlet Letter* and some of the tales. Noriguchi notes that "portions of Hawthorne's works often appear as part of English examinations for entry into Japanese universities" because "English teachers in Japan regard his works as ideal

3. See Fumio Ano, "Hawthorne Studies in Japan," 264–69; Kochi Doi et al., *Nihon No Eigaku 100 Nen-Meiji Hen: One Hundred Years of English Studies in Japan—The Meiji Era* (Tokyo: Kenkyusha, 1968), 117, 126; *A Bibliography of Translations of American Literary Works into Japanese, 1868–1967* (Tokyo: Harashobo, 1968); Koki Sato, "Hawthorne Accepted at Colleges and Universities," *Nathaniel Hawthorne Society of Japan Newsletter,* no. 6 (1987): 1–3; Junji Kunishige, "Hawthorne Studies in Japan, 1982–1985," *Nathaniel Hawthorne Society of Japan Newsletter,* no. 5 (1986): 12–13; Shinichiro Noriguchi, "Archetypal Symbolism in the Works of Nathaniel Hawthorne (Part 1)," *Fukuoka Women's Junior College Studies* 32 (1986): 33–56. See also Toshisaburo Koyama's Japanese translation of Henry James's *Hawthorne* (Tokyo: Nan'un-Do, 1964), which contains a bibliography of books and articles on Hawthorne published in Japan.

material for reading comprehension," and because his style "is based on the traditional English grammar, which Japanese secondary students are required to study. In addition, educators hope to cultivate their students' insight into human existence, which Hawthorne treats both profoundly and symbolically."[4] The authorities who chose him for this role may have thought the decision justified by the fact that Hawthorne held then, as he does now, a position of great importance in the American literary canon, but the choice seems also to have been due at least in part to the fact that, as Noriguchi implies, Hawthorne was thought to possess a classic English prose style eminently suitable for student imitation. The fact that this apparently limpid, neoclassical prose style concealed or permitted so much complexity and obscurity—so many difficulties and ambiguities—may, however, have delayed the appearance of his works in Japanese, for the authorities agree that his work was not read for its literary qualities until much later, ostensibly because it seemed too gloomy for Japanese tastes, was too much concerned with religious matters, and, interestingly, seemed too "difficult" to translate. The first stories ("David Swan" and "Fancy's Show Box") were not translated, in fact, until 1889—but with their appearance, a process of assimilation was begun that has continued to this day. As Fumio Ano has noted, most of the stories and two of the romances had been translated by 1975, at which time Hawthorne was second only to Poe in the overall number of translations of the works of American authors. By all accounts, too, the quality and sophistication of the translations has improved with time (and it may be worth noting, in this context, that there has been nothing comparable in the United States, in terms of interest in or appropriation of the classics of Japanese literature).

When the early translators began to approach Hawthorne's tales and sketches, they tended, as Koki Sato has pointed out, to avoid those with overtly religious themes, and especially those in which Hawthorne dealt with Christian concepts relating to sin and its consequences. This may have been due in part to the fact that the works were most often translated for and read by children, although even such potentially disturbing tales as "The Minister's Black Veil," and "Fancy's Show Box" (which, as Sato notes, are among those that "have long been liked

4. Shinichiro Noriguchi, "Archetypal Symbolism in the Works of Nathaniel Hawthorne (Part 1)," 33.

by the Japanese people") were most often treated as juvenile literature.[5] The varying number of translations of different tales and sketches seems in itself to reveal something about the tastes and preferences of a Japanese audience that was gradually creating its own image of Hawthorne—and here again I rely primarily on Professor Ano's research for the statistics on the number of translations. As I already noted, "David Swan" has long been a favorite of Japanese readers, and by 1967 there had been seven different translations of this slight tale—but also seven of "The Great Stone Face" (the first in 1892), and as many of "The Ambitious Guest" (the first in 1906). *The Scarlet Letter,* understandably, has been translated most often, the first of eleven different versions making its appearance in 1903. A number of tales that modern American critics consider to be of particular importance, however, have been given less attention: the first (and, as of 1967, the only) translations of "Rappaccini's Daughter" and "Young Goodman Brown," for example, appeared in 1948 and 1966, respectively; *The House of the Seven Gables* was first translated in 1964; and as late as 1975 there had been no translations of *The Blithedale Romance, The Marble Faun,* or the complete *Mosses from an Old Manse.* It may also be worth noting that it is clear that the tide of translations has ebbed and flowed in response to economic, ideological, political, and even military factors: when we look for first translations of individual works, for example, we find nothing between 1896 and 1902; only one item (*A Wonder Book*) between 1908 and 1924; nothing between 1935 and 1947; and only one story ("The Three Golden Apples") translated for the first time between 1952 and 1963.

Historically, then, readers in Japan and America have differed in their sense of the relative importance of various works, although of late there has been a steady convergence of critical interest. It seems clear that in Japan the early popularity of certain works was a function of their perceived "simplicity," which made them seem appropriate for use by students and, perhaps, facilitated translation. Gradually, however, Japanese academics began to study and analyze the works that had hitherto been unknown in Japan, or employed only as texts for learning English, and by the end of the nineteenth century biographical and critical material on Hawthorne also began to appear in textbooks

5. Kōki Sato, "Hawthorne Accepted at Colleges and Universities," 1.

used at Tokyo University and elsewhere. Seminal figures such as Lafcadio Hearn helped to establish a tradition of American literary studies with belletristic lectures on Poe and other American authors, although the first college and university lectures on Hawthorne and his works seem not to have been given until after the commencement of the Taisho era (1912–26). In the wake of such lectures, however, the development of original work on Hawthorne by Japanese scholars became inevitable.[6]

Our interest in the opinions that Japanese scholars might develop in regard to Hawthorne's work reflects a larger historical concern with the way other cultures have tended to view our own. As the reforms of the Meiji period in Japan commenced, American attitudes on the subject (reflecting our own sense of cultural insecurity) tended to be patronizing. Thus the tone of Ralph Waldo Emerson's "Address" at a banquet given at the Revere House in Boston on 2 August 1872 embodies something of the barely covert condescension and arrogance with which Americans of his day (exposed, especially after Commodore Perry's expedition to Japan in 1854, to an increasing flood of articles on Japan in popular magazines such as *Harper's Monthly*) tended to regard Japan and Japanese culture. Noting that the Japanese thought very highly of education, Emerson spoke of the "singular selection" this nation had showed "in appealing to America for its guidance and assistance in western civilization." The "brave and simple manner in which it has sent its pupils, its young men, to our schools and colleges and to learn our arts," he maintained,

> is a great honor to their wisdom and their noble heart. There is humanity as well as there is ambition. . . . And I have to say that I think the American government and American history owes great thanks to the enlightened policy of President Fillmore who, in 1852, sent Commodore Perry to that country and introduced a new thought into his embassy. Instead of sending to what he supposed a comparatively foreign and unrelated country, to say the least, to the civil nations—instead of sending to them beads

6. In a recent essay entitled "Imagination of Poe and Hawthorne," published in *Nathaniel Hawthorne Society of Japan Newsletter*, no. 8 (1989), Shinji Takuwa quotes from Hearn's lecture on "American Literature" given at Tokyo Imperial University in 1898: "I think that the imaginative part of literature is not only important, but that it is the only part of foreign literature which can be of real benefit to you" (page 1).

> and rum barrels, he sent the best of our civilization. He sent the very best instruments and inventions that the country could command. He sent the steamboat. He sent the telescope. He sent the telegraph. He sent all those instruments which had lately attracted and strengthened western civilization. This gift was gratefully and nobly received, instantly understood and remade in that country.[7]

Eventually, as we have seen, the "gift" would include American literature and thus the works of Hawthorne, encountered in the United States by the young Japanese students and scholars who had been sent there to acquire a Western education. American scholars, too, were understandably curious as to how their Japanese counterparts would "understand and remake" American culture as they did American technology. The attitude of American academics—more sophisticated, perhaps, than that of the elderly Emerson, but still revealing in its implicitly patronizing tone—is conveyed in several of the essays contained in a volume entitled *America to Japan: A Symposium of Papers by Representative Citizens of the United States on the Relations between Japan and America and on the Common Interests of the Two Countries* (1915), edited by Lindsay Russell in his capacity as president of the Japan Society of New York.[8] In "The Link of Literature," C. Alphonso Smith, then Poe Professor of English at the University of Virginia, suggested that it was advisable that a shared or international literature should be developed as a means of ensuring a "permanent fund of common traits and enduring ideals" to be held in common by the civilized nations of the world. Such literature, Smith opined, would link "nation to nation and people to people in a bond of common ideals and common sympathies," and in this context he invoked the "brilliant lectures delivered before the University of Virginia by Dr. Inazo Nitobé [*sic*], the Japanese Exchange Professor for 1911–1912," of which "none made so deep an impression, none so endeared the name of the speaker, and none so touched the elemental impulses of the hearers, as . . . an impromptu address on Edgar Allan Poe."[9] Europe, Smith went on to say, had long

7. Ralph Waldo Emerson, "Address at Japanese Banquet, August 2, 1872," in *Uncollected Writings: Essays, Addresses, Poems, Reviews and Letters* (New York: Lamb Publishing Company, 1912), 15–16.

8. *America to Japan: A Symposium of Papers by Representative Citizens of the United States on the Relations between Japan and America and on the Common Interests of the Two Countries,* ed. Lindsay Russell (New York: G. P. Putnam's Sons, 1915).

9. C. Alphonso Smith, "The Link of Literature," in *America to Japan,* 195–96.

since arrived at its own idea as to what "Americanism" meant by reading "Franklin, Jefferson, Irving, Cooper, Poe, Hawthorne, Longfellow, Emerson, Bret Harte, Mark Twain, and Walt Whitman," who "not only express with varying fullness the national spirit but are in a very real sense the ambassadors from the New World to the Old. . . . To understand them, to commune with them, to appraise their excellencies and their limitations, to realize that consciously or unconsciously they are exponents of Americanism," he wrote, "is to know what America is and what it stands for." The relevance of this for Japan was obvious: "Japan," Smith concludes,

> is already a reader, and an appreciative reader, of the best American literature, but she has not yet contributed to the interpretation of American literature. We do not associate Japan with our literature as we associate France, Germany, and of course Great Britain. These nations have contributed constructive criticism and have linked their literary thought with our own. But we need to be linked to Japan in the same sort of literary interchange. No literature can longer afford to be hemispherical. The symbol of the twentieth century is the sphere, not the hemisphere. American literature is not hemispherical in its appeal but it is hemispherical in its utilization of foreign criticism. It needs the Oriental note.[10]

Implicit in Smith's speech is the idea that the study of nineteenth-century American literature was to be promoted (as others would promote the introduction of Christianity into Japan) in order to encourage a cultural shift from traditional to Western modes of thought in what had hitherto been a closed (and, as the implication so often was, a "primitive") Japanese society. Such a shift, it was thought, would help to bring Japan into the community of "civilized" nations. Not all voices, however, were so implicitly insulting: in "Japan's Literary Relations with the United States" (another essay in the same volume), for example, George Haven Putnam commented on the study of American literature by Japanese students during the late nineteenth century, and noted that, to America's shame, there was little interest in Japanese literature in America, although there was a large demand for American literature in Japan.

10. C. Alphonso Smith, "The Link of Literature," 196–97.

Hawthorne has maintained his position in Japan as an author worthy of study, it seems to me, in part because Japanese scholars have concluded that his works are not only classics of world literature, but crucial to an understanding of the period that we still refer to as the American literary renaissance. There may also, however, be other reasons for his continued popularity. It would be interesting to speculate about the ways in which the sensibilities of Nathaniel Hawthorne, that eminent descendant of New England Puritans, might have much in common with attitudes and affinities—spiritual or psychological—that we might think of as being traditionally Japanese. We might read "Egotism; or, The Bosom-Serpent," for example, as a nineteenth-century rationalist version of the archetypal Western story of demonic possession, and compare it with similar Japanese tales that center on the ancient belief that the fox spirit has the power to possess or bewitch the unwary, especially since the sources for Hawthorne's tale include a historical reference to a Connecticut boy who, during the witchcraft times, was believed to be possessed because he could no longer speak, but only bark like a fox. Hawthorne's interest in masks and outer appearances was perhaps occasioned by the fact that his birthplace (as the museums of the city reveal to this day) was one of the great centers of American trade with the Far East. There is also the issue of his preoccupation with his ancestors, and the mingled sense of pride, duty, guilt, and resentment that characterized his attitude toward them. All these traits might strike a responsive chord in many Japanese readers, and, in fact, Japanese scholars have shown marked interest in the changes that Hawthorne's years in England and in Italy made upon him—in his plight as a man both fascinated and repulsed by his immersion in the older, alien cultures that made it increasingly difficult for him to retain his sense of personal identity. A number of Japanese scholars seem also to have concluded that Hawthorne's work contains unique insights into the nature of America itself; that it expresses, perhaps, as no American author before or since has done so well, something of the ambiguity inherent in the American (and the human) experience.

Part of Hawthorne's attraction for Japanese scholars may be the assumption that Hawthorne's interest in what Henry James referred to as "the deeper psychology" makes him particularly useful as a guide or tutor for those scholars who are interested (as many Japanese scholars certainly are) in the contours of the American psyche. Thus, we might expect that a work such as *The Scarlet Letter*—in which Hester Prynne's refusal to submit to the dictates of an oppressive society is both praised and condemned—might be expected to be of particular interest because of the cultural differences it embodies, differences not merely between the America of the Puritans and Hawthorne's Victorian America (or our own), but between the very different cultures of America and Japan. The Hawthorne scholars of Japan are interested in him, too, not merely because of his work, but because there is something in the personality that he managed to convey in his work that seems to strike a chord of "sympathy"—a word that, in Hawthorne's day, implied something much deeper than it does today.

On occasion, one does seem to encounter a distinctively Japanese perspective in the Japanese Hawthorne scholarship that has appeared in English—although only rarely, perhaps because the conventions and constraints that govern the form are those of the traditional (and, in most cases, rather impersonal) American or British scholarly essay. We may encounter such hints more readily, it seems to me, in less formal discourses—as in the following excerpt from Tatsuru Iwasaki's presentation on "My Kinsman, Major Molineux" (given at the Fourth Annual Conference of the Nathaniel Hawthorne Society of Japan in Tokyo in 1985) in which he wrestles, as so many of us have done, with the problem of Robin Molineux's laughter:

> [The story] has two or three marvellous things in it, and the most marvellous thing appears in the last scene, where Robin, the hero, who comes from the country to a town to visit his kinsman, laughs at him. Robin's laughter sounds marvellous and unnatural to me, for my careless reading prevents me from finding any clear reasons why he laughs such a laugh. Indeed it is very marvellous to laugh at his kinsman whom he respects so much and moreover who is in "the circumstance of overwhelming humiliation"! Robin's laughter is marvellous and unnatural.
>
> So I am trying to solve this question by borrowing the theory of Otaya Miyagi, a psychologist, and by considering the meaning of Hawthorne's "Romance."[11]

11. Tatsuru Iwasaki, "My Kinsman, Major Molineux," a paper given at the Fourth Annual Conference of the Nathaniel Hawthorne Society of Japan in Tokyo in 1985, and quoted in *Nathaniel Hawthorne Society of Japan Newsletter*, no. 5 (1986): 8–9.

There is a modesty here that is itself rare in American literary scholarship, and a hint that Iwasaki's difficulties may stem in part from the fact that a young man in Japan would never have reacted in this fashion had he encountered a respected and elderly kinsman in such a situation. It may be revealing that, in my own experience, American university students of the present day are much less likely to be troubled by Robin's behavior, which they may even see as sensible, given the circumstances.

We may find a similar hint in the fact that room is still found in Japanese literary journals for accounts of literary pilgrimages of the sort that are no longer in vogue in America (although they have long been more acceptable among American Hawthornians and Melvillians than among scholars in other fields). Japanese scholars now visit Sleepy Hollow Cemetery in Concord or Hawthorne's birthplace in Salem in much the same spirit in which Victorian Americans on the Grand Tour used to flock to the cultural holy places of Great Britain and Europe—they came as tourists, to be sure, but also, in many cases, to express respect for and sympathy with the dead author, and in hopes of catching a restorative glimpse of his (or her) lost world. Thus in his "Fiction as a Whole," Yoshio Isaka notes that on the last day of 1982 he sat down to meditate on the steps of Salem City Hall, just as "the Old Year" in Hawthorne's "The Sister Years" had done long before him (and as few inhabitants of the Salem of the present day, perhaps, would ever think of doing). It was in this same mood that Hawthorne himself went to Uttoxeter marketplace, to stand on the spot where Samuel Johnson had stood to punish himself for having offended his father many years before. In his "Hawthorne's England, My England," Mayumi Kurosaki informs us that in 1982 he had an opportunity to visit Hawthorne's "Old Home," where—possessed of "little money and little time," but imbued with "deep emotion"—he followed the ancestral footsteps through Liverpool, Stratford-on-Avon, Old Boston, Oxford, London, and elsewhere, noting that he "wore out two pairs of shoes in two months," and concluding that Hawthorne must have been "quite a strong walker." Kurosaki was surprised and saddened, however, by the fact that the English showed little interest in Hawthorne: "During my stay in England, I met no Englishman, excepting professors of literature, who knew the American writer." In his "Serendipity in Plymouth, New Hampshire," Fumio Ano describes his experiences during a tour of Hawthorne-related sites in Maine and New Hampshire, in the course of which he had better luck in encountering fellow Hawthornians. Ichitaro Toma's "An Excursion into Hawthorne's World" discusses the ways in which various talismanic artifacts—relics of the Old Province-House, for example—still preserved in museums at the Peabody Essex Museum and the Massachusetts Historical Society "enable us to imagine ourselves strolling through Hawthorne's world," and goes on to recall the author's visit to England, where he was able to view the "Martyr's Chamber" at Poulton Hall (which found its way into *Dr. Grimshawe's Secret*) and meditate over the famous bloody footprint at Smithills Hall.[12]

For various reasons, the Hawthorne scholars of Japan have become so numerous and so prolific of late that, as Sato has commented, "so many papers are read and so many essays are written on Hawthorne that we cannot keep up with all of them."[13] In 1986, Kunishige noted that "More than 50 monographs on Hawthorne are written every year."[14] The Nathaniel Hawthorne Society of Japan is the second largest in the world, smaller only than its American counterpart, and recently its brief *Newsletter* underwent a transformation, emerging as the *Forum*, in which full-length papers have begun to appear for the first time. There is something of the same interest in Melville, whose Pequod touched Japanese waters, and a similar and longstanding preoccupation with Poe and with Faulkner, but the attraction of Hawthorne, who has always both appalled and enticed his readers, runs deeper.

It may seem presumptuous (and it is certainly dangerous) to permit myself these speculations on the nature of the relationship between Hawthorne and Japanese scholars, and particularly so since I am not now (and cannot, in the natural course of things, ever hope to become) an expert in the matter at hand. What follows, then, is a sampling of Japanese Hawthorne criticism that has been published since 1975, assembled here, as I have already suggested, in order to provide American scholars with some sense of the range of scholarly interests,

12. See Yoshio Isaka, "Fiction as a Whole," *Nathaniel Hawthorne Society of Japan Newsletter,* no. 6 (1987): 7–8; Mayumi Kurosaki, "Hawthorne's England, My England," *Nathaniel Hawthorne Society of Japan Newsletter,* no. 6 (1987): 8–9; Fumio Ano, "Serendipity in Plymouth, New Hampshire," *Nathaniel Hawthorne Society of Japan Newsletter,* no. 8 (1989): 4–5; and Ichitaro Toma, "An Excursion into Hawthorne's World," *Nathaniel Hawthorne Society of Japan Newsletter,* no. 8 (1989): 2–3.

13. Koki Sato, "Hawthorne Accepted at Colleges and Universities," 3.

14. Junji Kunishige, "Hawthorne Studies in Japan, 1982–1985," 12.

ideologies, and critical methodologies employed by their Japanese counterparts during recent years.

Keisuke Kawakubo, "What Can We Learn from Hawthorne? (1)," *Bulletin of Reitaku University*, no. 20 (1975): 1–14. Kawakubo discusses the meaning that Hawthorne studies have had in his own life, as well as the role that a familiarity with Hawthorne's works might be assumed to play in the "welfare of the general public." He suggests that although Hawthorne was neither "a scholar of ethics nor a moral philosopher," moral values were important to him, and the elucidation of those values is an important function of the critic. One such value derives from the sort of "poetic insight" that—born as it was out of Hawthorne's mature awareness of the complexities and ambiguities of life—insured that pessimism would be more readily apparent in his work than the optimism shared by so many of his contemporaries. Kawakubo informs us, however, that Hawthorne believed that the artist who is possessed of the "sadly gifted eye," which permits insight into the secret sins of others, but also imbues the artist with love and sympathy for his fellows, will be both wise and happy—although to avail oneself of this gift of insight is to be "in a sense, meddlesome, unpleasant, and in bad taste." Another of Hawthorne's significant moral themes is the importance of living as a part of what he called "the whole sympathetic chain of human nature": cut off from this chain, isolated by pride or selfishness, Hawthornean protagonists turn to stone, or become "the Outcast of the Universe." And although Hawthorne did not believe in moral perfectibility, Kawakubo notes that he did believe that the perfecting of one's moral character was "the most essential goal in life."

Nobunao Matsuyama, "'Faces' of Hawthorne's Young Goodman Brown," *Doshisha Studies in English Language and Literature*, no. 10 (1975): 52–53. Matsuyama notes that although Hawthorne says nothing about Brown's physiognomy, Brown, in fact, possesses various "metaphorical" faces. The appearance of his mother at the witches' Sabbat, warning him to avoid the step he is about to take, and the evidence suggesting that he has been overly dependent upon other women (first Goody Cloyse, and then his wife, Faith) for his spiritual instruction, reveals that he wears the face of the child who has never matured in an emotional sense. A number of his other faces represent aspects of Puritan thought: one, for example, is that of the typical resident of Salem Village during the witch hysteria, and another is that of the "narrow-minded puritan" who cannot comprehend the ambiguous nature of good and evil. (In this sense, Matsuyama suggests, Brown's is the "reverse" of the face worn by Hilda in *The Marble Faun.*) Most importantly, given the "historical situation" of the work, Brown's face is that of a third-generation Puritan, "much reduced in religious ardor and moral chastity." And finally, given his inability to acknowledge his own moral corruption (which he views in terms of the pact with the Devil), his final face is that of a "pseudo-Faust."

Hiroshi Noro, "The Reverend Arthur Dimmesdale in *The Scarlet Letter,*" *Bulletin of Shokei Women's Junior College,* no. 22 (October 1975): 57–63. Noro, a Christian who believes that the Bible is "God's own infallible word," emphasizes the importance of the confession theme in the romance (particularly as revealed in the three scaffold scenes), and examines the probable efficacy of Dimmesdale's final confession in the light of biblical teachings.

Yoshitaka Aoyama, "'Rappaccini's Daughter': The Garden as a 'Neutral Territory,'" *Sophia English Studies* 1 (1976): 37–52. Aoyama focuses on the significance of the garden itself as the environment in which the story takes place. (The term "environment" is used here in a very broad sense, as Richard Poirier employed it in *A World Elsewhere.*) Invoking the insights of a number of American and British critics, Aoyama suggests that Hawthorne's famous "neutral territory" was a state of mind, an eternal realm within which he could examine his own "burdened soul." In this "mediating space between social space and private, inner space," Aoyama argues, Hawthorne sought "his freedom and his form"—and it was in this "self-contained, self-governing, self-sufficient" world of "verbal space," this "playfield of the imagination," that dramas such as "Rappaccini's Daughter," are set. The complex interactions of Giovanni, Beatrice, and Dr. Rappaccini reveal the inevitable failure of the artist who seeks to gain eternity through his art, but finds that he cannot escape from the actual world.

Takahiro Kamogawa, "Textual Editing of the Centenary *Marble Faun,*" *Kyushu American Literature,* no. 17 (1976): 42–65. Kamogawa suggests that, although the various volumes of the Centenary Edition of Hawthorne's works have been "reviewed, praised, censured, or criticised," they have not been "properly assessed" in terms of the "editorial treatment of the bibliographical evidence," and he presents his own paper as "an attempt to assess the degree of success in the establishment of the definitive text in *The Marble Faun* and to propose revisions to it." The essay is, in fact, a sophisticated and perceptive critique of the methodology employed by the editors of the Centenary Edition. Kamogawa proposes a revision of their "defective" practices—necessary, in his opinion, because they defined authorial intention too narrowly in a text that was written and published under "extraordinary circumstances." Decisions made on the basis of statistical evidence, Kamogawa insists, cannot be justified if they do not sufficiently account for Hawthorne's own inconsistent but deliberate attempts to anglicize or antiquate his spellings, his limited knowledge of Italian, his careless proofreading of his own text, Sophia Hawthorne's alterations of (or "overintervention" in) the copy-text manuscript, later compositorial sophistication, and still later editorial emendation, modernization, and "normalization" of punctuation, spelling, capitalization, etc. In essence, then, the essay—which argues for a version of Hawthorne's text that would be less obviously "consistent" but that would in its very inconsistency approximate more closely the text he actually produced—reminds us that any text is a complex conflating of various intentions: those of the editors and of the critic/reader himself no less than those of Hawthorne. We are reminded of the difficulties of such analysis (and of the pitfalls that await the most careful of proofreaders) when we note that at one point in the essay the title of Hawthorne's romance appears as *The Mrble Faun.*

Takahiro Kamogawa, "*The Marble Faun,* A Novelized Journal?" in *Bulletin of the Faculty of Education, Kagoshima University* (1976): 22–23 (English summary). Kamogawa suggests that *The Marble Faun* may be best understood in the context of the literary genre to which it belongs—the "journal in the form of a novel," or the "novelized journal," related both to the classic Victorian travel journal and the traditional guidebook. Viewing the work as a novel rather than as a romance, Kamogawa points out that its subject matter and basic themes derive from journal entries Hawthorne made during his travels in Italy in 1858–59. The entries on Praxiteles's famous statue of a faun (which turned out to be a copy) and the equally famous portrait of Beatrice Cenci (then attributed to Guido Reni) provide the "central axis of the thematic structure" of the novel, permitting analogies to be drawn between the attributes and traits displayed by the four central characters. Although the fact that the work is set in various locales reflects "the popular taste of the day," permitting Hawthorne to indulge in detailed descriptions of the sites that all tourists were expected to visit, it exerts a "centrifugal, loosening, and therefore damaging influence" on the underlying structure. The journal entries from which he quarried the edifice of *The Marble Faun* finally make it clear that while Hawthorne imbued all objects with a moral significance, he tended to regard works of art from a literary point of view, and historical objects from a personal one.

Shinichiro Noriguchi, "Allegory in Hawthorne's Short Stories," *Kyushu American Literature* 16 (1976): 66–74. "Allegory," Noriguchi writes, "is the key to the world of Hawthorne's writing." While contemporaries such as Emerson and Thoreau extolled the virtues of self-confidence, optimism, and self-emancipation, Hawthorne led an isolated life, probing the inner workings of the human heart and thinking of himself as a "psychological romancer." He owed his propensity for allegory to his childhood reading of Bunyan and Spenser and the Puritan atmosphere in which he was brought up, and deliberately adopted the "allegorical style" of his favorite eighteenth-century authors. Allegory itself permitted him to express "more profound meanings" than realistic literature could, and at the same time it made it possible for him to criticize both the Puritanism of his ancestors and the materialism of his own day, while continuing to explore the depths of the human heart. In the allegorical tale "The Celestial Rail-road," a satirical treatment of transcendentalism, Hawthorne created an updated Bunyan's *Pilgrim's Progress*—if he were writing it today, Noriguchi suggests, he might have called it "The Celestial Airline." Hawthorne's disparaging description of the train (which Noriguchi sees as "one of the most convenient facilities that science has ever produced") suggests that he "seems not to have admired such scientific modernization." In "The Minister's Black Veil," Hawthorne presents Mr. Hooper as a "monster" produced by Puritanism, who "egocentrically lives by an idea rather than by warm human love." Hooper's certainty that everyone else has sinned thus makes him a sinner himself. "The Birthmark" blends Puritan notions about the universality of original sin with a critique of nineteenth-century materialism and arrogant "modern" science, a theme that is also emphasized in "Rappaccini's Daughter." Both Edgar Allan Poe and Henry James deplored Hawthorne's tendency toward allegory, but

Noriguchi asserts that Hawthorne's tales have become more and more popular precisely because allegory "appeals most to the reader." Hawthorne himself, as Arlin Turner has pointed out, did not think of allegory as "an inferior literary form," and in this case, Noriguchi maintains, his opinion was correct, since, given his habits of thought and the nature of his creative processes, he would not have been able to explore the "dark places of the human heart" without it.

Motoo Takigawa, "The Relationship between God and Human Beings in American Literature," *Studies in English Literature* 53 (1976): 59–73 (English summary in *Studies in English Literature* 54 [1977]: 219–20). Takigawa suggests that although in *The Scarlet Letter* Hawthorne made the first great American attempt to create "the image of a human being coping with God Almighty," his attempt was an ambiguous one, since he balanced the "awe and terror" he felt before God with the "praise and wonder" he devoted to the all-too-human Hester. The individual who insists on establishing a relationship with God only on his or her own terms would recur in American literature—in Melville's Ahab, Faulkner's Dilsey, and Hemingway's Santiago, for example—but after the Second World War, American authors could no longer comprehend the "terror and torture" that Hawthorne and Melville endured when they confronted the "non-existence" of their God, who nevertheless seemed much stronger than the "weak and fragile" demigod who remained to Faulkner or Hemingway. Yet the work of William Styron, Flannery O'Connor, or Richard Bach reveals that Americans will always search for new ways to articulate their sense of the relationship between God and man.

Keisuke Kawakubo, "Hawthorne: Encounters between America and Europe," *Bulletin of Reitaku University,* no. 23 (1977): 7–26. Early in his career, Kawakubo contends, Hawthorne shared the traditional perspective of American authors, many of whom (motivated by a degree of "self-love and egotism") saw themselves as a new "Chosen People" and their own country as the New Jerusalem, while they portrayed Europe as a place of hellish corruption. (They did so, Kawakubo contends, because America is "an artificially invented country" that needs "invented myths of national origin"—which may prove destructive. "Any proud nation, any proud individual," he notes, "shall suffer the nemesis of pride. Therefore, beware, America! and beware, Japan!") A certain degree of xenophobia may be reflected, for example, in the fact that Hawthorne's villains tend to be foreign-born (a characteristic of the Gothic genre, in any case) while his "wholesome, fair-haired maidens are New Englanders"; on the whole, he associates things American with good, light, and innocence, things European with evil, darkness, and experience.

Kawakubo goes on to examine *The English Notebooks, Our Old Home,* and *The Marble Faun* in order to reveal the ways in which Hawthorne's sojourn in Europe affected his perspective on such matters. Various notebook entries (and the essays in *Our Old Home* derived from them) reveal that Hawthorne's attitude toward England was "complex and ambivalent"—although he felt a strong sense of nostalgia and a deep appreciation of the English landscape, he was irritated by the patronizing "arrogance and condescending attitude" of many of the "British Philistines" (as Matthew Arnold called them) whom he encountered there. In *The Marble Faun,* the innocence that the formula demands of the Americans is shared by Donatello, who then falls, fortunately or otherwise. Hilda, symbolic of the "uprooted and rootless American," is also innocent, but her very innocence is portrayed as a kind of flaw, for it renders her incapable of enduring moral evil or of sympathizing with sinners. Hilda falls, in a sense, when she becomes aware of the crime committed by Miriam and Donatello, but the experience deepens her soul, as does her encounter with Roman Catholicism, although she leaves it behind in the end to return to America—as Hawthorne and his family did. Their experience, however, had changed them: in Kawakubo's opinion, they had themselves fallen, having "eaten of the fruit of knowledge too deeply," so that they became "divided selves, torn between the two sides of the Atlantic." Hawthorne himself, in particular, was "unbound from the myth of America," and in his later years we can observe "with awe and sympathy the painful struggle of an intellectual who devoted himself to a better understanding of two cultures."

Masayuki Matsushita, "A Study of *The House of the Seven Gables:* Its Structure of Time (1)," *Bulletin of the College of General Education, Tokushima University* (1977): 93 (English summary). Because "a bygone time" exerts so heavy an influence on "the very present" in *The House of the Seven Gables,* Matsushita comments, we tend not to realize how brief is the span of "actual" time that makes up the "present" of the romance—and considering Hawthorne's reticence on the subject, it is difficult to determine how much time actually passes.

Masayuki Matsushita, "A Study of *The House of the Seven Gables:* Its Structure of Time (2)," *Bulletin of the College of General Education, Tokushima University* (1978): 49–66. In this, the second part of his essay, Matsushita examines the first two days described in *The House of the Seven Gables,* a period that he considers to be a "model of a pattern which governs all the rest of the work." "Present" time begins in chapter 2 —the first chapter being given over to a history of the six preceding generations of Pyncheons and Maules—and the events described in chapters 2 through 4 all take place during the course of one day, while the events that take place during the second day are described in chapters 5 and 6. Matsushita notes that when we use a day as a basic unit of measurement, certain similarities emerge in the two clusters of chapters, each of which is divided into three or four sections: "early morning before breakfast, forenoon before dinner, and afternoon and evening or night." This, he claims, is a "ruling pattern which helps to give reality" to the romance.

Satoshi Okabe, "Nathaniel Hawthorne's Attitude toward Literary Creation," *Bulletin of the Tohoku Institute of Technology* (1978) (English summary). Okabe subdivides Hawthorne's creative process into three parts: "perception, his world of vision, and expression." He outlines first that Hawthorne valued material objects not for their external appearance, but for what they suggested to him while he was in the passive state of mind that, eliminating "obtrusive actualities," permitted him to apprehend or assign moral meanings. It was while in this hypnagogic state in which he could enter the "moonlit world" of the imagination, Okabe maintains, that Hawthorne engaged in creative activities, although he knew that it was dangerous (in a psychological sense) to remain there too long. When it came to the expression of his conceits, Hawthorne's problem lay in the difficulties he experienced in attempting to give the appearance of "warm reality" to his visionary creations, and his solution lay in his decision to adopt the "neutral territory" of the romance as his literary form.

Fumio Ano, "Hawthorne's View of the Indian: Chiefly about 'The Duston Family,'" *Tohoku Studies in American Literature* 1 (1979): 7–19 (English summary, 61–62). Ano contends that, although Hawthorne wrote that he was "shut out from the most peculiar field of American fiction, by an inability to see any romance, or poetry, or grandeur, or beauty in the Indian character, at least, till such traits were pointed out by others," and although in his stories the Indian appears most often as a devilish being lurking in the wilderness, this was an image derived from the Puritan treatment of the Indian, and does not recur in his sketches, where he characterizes the Indian as a human being possessed of "a mind, and a heart, and an immortal soul," and where the views expressed are, presumably, closer to those which he himself held. In "The Duston Family," for example, Hawthorne describes Indians in sympathetic terms while criticizing the frontier "heroine" Hannah Duston, inverting the way Cotton Mather had treated the same episode even as he drew heavily upon Mather's account. Ano suggests that Hawthorne's treatment of the episode may also reflect both his prejudice against Mather, whom he regarded as a bigot, and his distaste for Duston's bloodthirsty and unfeminine behavior.

Shizuo Asai, "*The House of the Seven Gables:* A Story of Time," *Studies in American Literature,* no. 16 (1979): 28–49. Most critics have seen the ending of *The House of the Seven Gables* as being either ironic (because, having inherited Jaffrey Pyncheon's fortune, Holgrave and the remaining Pyncheons may once again repeat the sins of the fathers) or as a failure (if Hawthorne himself, neglecting to notice this potential irony, intended it as a "happy" ending). Asai sees the "Governor Pyncheon" chapter as crucial to an understanding of the meaning of the ending, for in it there are two sorts of time—the personal time recorded by Jaffrey Pyncheon's watch, and the time measured by the "world-clock" that never ceases to beat. What we might refer to as "Pyncheon time" or "Pyncheon history" began, Asai argues, when the sun first shone on the new sundial on the newly constructed House of the Seven Gables, marking, in Hawthorne's words, "the passage of the first bright hour in a history, that was not destined to be all so bright." When Jaffrey's watch runs down and finally stops because he is dead and can no longer wind it, Pyncheon time—and the Pyncheon curse—have run their course. A genuinely "happy ending," then, is indicated, and it is reflected in the fact that, while the first four chapters of the romance are full of dark images, the final three are full of bright ones, as Holgrave and Phoebe, freed from the past, look to the bright future that has been denied to Jaffrey. The romance begins, as it were, in night, but ends in day—"daybreak" occurring in the break between the "Governor Pyncheon" chapter and the following "Alice's Posies" chapter. The "world-clock," however, continues to tick, and Asai concludes with the suggestion that Hawthorne gives no clue as to whether the future will be a happy one or not.

Takashi Sasaki, "Hawthorne and Brook Farm," *Doshisha American Studies*, no. 15 (March 1979) (English summary). In order to get a sense of Hawthorne's evolving attitude toward the possibility of social reform, Sasaki first examines the various letters that tell the tale of the young author's growing disillusionment with the communal experiment at Brook Farm, and then turns to works such as "Earth's Holocaust" and *The Blithedale Romance* for notions as to what Hawthorne thought he had learned from his utopian experience. The letters suggest that he took the whole project quite seriously at first, but grew weary and frustrated as his farm chores kept him from his books. Sasaki also finds in these letters a tendency toward an egotism "invariably incompatible with the spirit of fraternal community," something of which (as the character of Coverdale in *The Blithedale Romance* reveals) Hawthorne himself seems to have been well aware. Nevertheless, writes Sasaki, Brook Farm "struck deeply, and forever, into Hawthorne's consciousness," and he went on to reveal a preoccupation with "the theme of human progress and reform," not only in several sketches published in 1843 and 1844 but in *The Blithedale Romance* itself, printed ten years after he had left Brook Farm. His "sullen scepticism," Sasaki believes, led him to the conclusion that the individual must reform himself before institutional or environmental reform will be possible—an attitude that prevented him from becoming so active an advocate of reform as were contemporaries such as Ripley and Emerson.

Yoshitaka Aoyama, "History in *The House of the Seven Gables*," *Sophia English Studies* 5 (1980): 62–83. "The central image in *The House of the Seven Gables*," Aoyama proclaims, "is the house itself"—a *hortus conclusus*, a backwater of time, a gloomy labyrinth, a great human heart, veiled in mystery. It is also a prison, a dungeon, a kingdom of the past—one of the "Dead Men's houses," as Holgrave calls it—and a tomb, inhabited when the romance opens by characters who are little more than ghosts. The drama itself is "a larger version of the [puppet] play performed by an Italian boy," and Aoyama notes the preoccupation with the number seven—with its implications of both perfection and apocalypse—that underlies so much of the structure of the romance, hinting that the house functions too as a womb, a microcosm that (after Phoebe, all unaware, performs her "homely witchcraft") gives birth to a new Eden. Holgrave's nature inclines him to commit the unpardonable sin of exploiting Phoebe, but her love—and Judge Pyncheon's death—transform him. Clifford, possessed of a keen but passive imagination, discovers that he cannot flee from the past, and it is the passing and power of time itself that eventually brings about the "redemption of the past" in the death of Judge Pyncheon. In the end, however, Aoyama contends that *The House of the Seven Gables* must be considered a failure—not, as many critics have insisted, because of its ending or the weakness of its plot structure, but because all of the characters are caricatures: "extremely flat," "too weak for the theme," and lacking in the life with which Hawthorne managed to imbue the characters in his other completed romances.

Yoshitaka Aoyama, "A Pocket of Time: History and Utopia in *The Blithedale Romance*," *Studies in American Literature*, no. 17 (1980): 21–39. Aoyama maintains that a cynical Hawthorne, always skeptical of the possibility of reform, intended *The Blithedale Romance* as a dystopian novel. The Veiled Lady signifies the reality of Blithedale, hidden behind a veil of illusion: she would have rewarded those who approached her with "holy faith," but dooms those who approach her egotistically or in "scornful scepticism." All of the Blithedalers are masqueraders. Both Priscilla and Zenobia are Veiled Ladies; Hollingsworth promotes his own interests; Westervelt is an incarnation of death and corruption. Coverdale, too, has his secrets, but he is also the perceiver of realities and uncoverer of secrets, seeing "the backside of the universe" through his hotel-room window. And it is through his eyes, of course, that we observe the collapse of the doomed kingdom of the Blithedalers who, having stepped aside from history, find themselves to be outcasts of the universe, trapped in Hawthorne's "only one true grand tragedy."

Satoshi Okabe, "Hawthorne and England," *Tohoku Studies in American Literature*, no. 4 (1980) (English summary). Okabe argues that insufficient attention has been paid to the inner conflict that shaped Hawthorne's ambivalent attitude toward England. On the one hand, Hawthorne's mind and art were saturated with English influences, and he was attracted by "the restful atmosphere brought about by the cultural density of England," especially since he was disturbed by the "nerve-rackingly boisterous" America of his day, with its emphasis on progress and democracy; on the other hand, as a good American who felt something of the historical animosity that existed between the two nations, he was irritated by what he perceived as English arrogance and complacency. The anxiety that the American Civil War brought him made England seem even more attractive, and the resultant guilt helped to shape *The Ancestral Footstep* and *Doctor Grimshawe's Secret,* in which his American claimants reject English titles and estates "and participate in the building of a new civilization in America."

Shiro Yokozawa, "Nathaniel Hawthorne's Mental Attitude toward the Civil War," *Journal of the English Institute* 11 (1980): 83–85 (English summary, 183–85). The writing Hawthorne did at the Wayside upon returning to Concord after the start of the Civil War suggests that his genius was on the wane. Although it has been maintained that he had exhausted either his artistry or his health, Yokozawa proposes that there is strong evidence—in his abhorrence of the brutality and cruelty of battle, his attitude toward the problem of slavery, and his fears about the continued existence of the Union—that he was deeply troubled by the outbreak of the war itself, although he took the side of the North.

Keisuke Kawakubo, "Art and Artists in *The Marble Faun,*" *Bulletin of Reitaku University* 31 (1981): 1–25. Hawthorne's views on art are the subject of Kawakubo's essay, which focuses on the last completed romance as containing more of Hawthorne's ideas on art than do any of his other works. His stay in England had made him more conscious of pictorial art and more interested in the subject, Kawakubo submits, than he had ever been before—he visited the Manchester Arts Exhibition of 1857, for example, twelve or thirteen times between late July and early September. When the family removed to Italy, he found there a wealth of material for his new romance, in which three of the four main characters are artists of one sort or another. Miriam's powerful but disturbing paintings and sketches are her troubled expressions of things that haunt her. Hilda is a skilled copyist possessed of what Hawthorne refers to as a "sensitive faculty of appreciation," but after she witnesses Donatello's murder of Miriam's model she discovers that she has lost her sympathy for art, so that when she looks at a painting she sees "but a crust of paint over an emptiness." Her insight revives and deepens, however, after her confession at St. Peter's, although—again in Hawthorne's words—"it is questionable whether she was ever so perfect a copyist, thenceforth." Kenyon is a cool and dispassionate sculptor, a seeker after perfection who despises his own work, and who, with Hilda, clings to the legacy of New England Puritanism in the midst of the "brilliant illusion" of Roman Catholic art. Kawakubo contends that Hawthorne's view of art was "Romantic and Neo-platonic"; that he was disturbed by the burden of the past embodied in European ruins; and that he made a conscientious effort to learn as much as possible about European art, becoming acquainted in the process with a number of American expatriate artists in Rome and Florence. The net result of all of this exposure, Kawakubo claims, is that Hawthorne's artistic sensibilities became "more flexible," while his "understanding of the old civilization became wider and deeper."

Seyichiro Ueno, "The Scarlet Letter *A* for America?" in *Kyushu American Literature* 22 (1981): 32–39. Ueno notes that Hawthorne commands "the art of mystification," and then speculates that the scarlet *A* stands for America. He asks why the story is a "sombre" one, and establishes that it is because there can be no rebirth, no possibility of fleeing from America for the sinner Hester, whose dream of rebirth becomes a path of resignation. Dimmesdale, too, dreams of a rebirth that he is to achieve by escaping from America, and transforms himself into a transcendentalist. His election sermon is "a patriotic homage to 'Manifest Destiny,'" but there is an undertone of pathos—at that point, he is well aware that his optimistic vision of the future is a mirage. Hawthorne may have intended the appearance of the meteor to signify that "America's destiny shall be as brief as a meteor." Hester, a type of Hawthorne, returns to America in the end, to devote herself to art "in this artistically barren ground," but Pearl does not—perhaps Hawthorne repudiates her, not trusting her with the future of America because her father is the transcendentalist Dimmesdale. Perhaps, however, Pearl will return eventually, having absorbed civilization in Europe. Like Hester, Hawthorne remains in America (for the time) because he is guilty and must expiate his sin. *The Scarlet Letter,* then, is a great jeremiad, criticizing American materialism and Puritanism—the story of the destiny or doom of the American artist planted in ground artistically barren. (A later version of this essay appeared in volume thirty-two of *Studies in English Language and Literature* [1982].)

Seyichiro Ueno, "The Scarlet Letter *A* for America: What Hester Prynne Wears," *Studies in English Language and Literature* 32 (1982): 101–

2 (English summary). Ueno argues that Hawthorne was a great and elusive artist—an allegorist or symbolist whose work is perhaps best approached through a hermeneutic process. In this sense, Ueno reads Hawthorne very much as Melville and Poe did: as an author whose works contain unsuspected depths. He sees Hester Prynne, for example, as being so mysterious a character that "critics have avoided discussing her in proportion to her status," and defines her as a "dark 'Columbia'": the personification of the continent of North America as the Indian Queen, the Indian Princess, and the Dark Lady had been before her, an American symbol of Mother Earth. Dimmesdale is seen as a man who loses the American Dream, and the Scarlet Letter represents America itself, so that when Hester wears it she gives expression to Hawthorne's quest for the meaning of America—a quest that involves him in a critique of transcendentalism. Ueno's is an essay with a strong sense of the breadth of the received tradition of Western scholarship relating to these issues—he cites, for example, D. H. Lawrence, Phillip Young, Leslie Fiedler, Joshua C. Taylor, Henry James, Edwin Fussell, Michael D. Bell, Sacvan Bercovitch, Henry Nash Smith, Perry Miller, and Rudolph Von Abele.

Masahiro Nakamura, "Hawthorne's English Romance: The Return of a Homeless American," *Chu-Shikoku Studies in American Literature,* no. 19 (June 1983): 60–69. Nakamura examines the three unfinished English romances and the ways in which the plot and structure of each (or the lack of plot and structure) may be seen as recording the attempts of an enfeebled and frustrated Hawthorne to come to terms with his own confused attitudes toward his homeland and his "Old Home."

Noboru Saito, "Hawthorne's Attitude in Observing England," *Rissho University Studies in English Literature,* no. 11 (1983): 13–26. It is Saito's contention that Nathaniel Hawthorne was not influenced by the "Frontier Spirit," but stood aloof from the pursuit of "things American," never freeing himself completely from "the range of vision and emotional restriction of English literature." It was the fact that, although he lived in a land with only "a short history," he had chosen to write romances (in which "the importance is attached to the past rather than to the present"), Saito suggests, that gave Hawthorne's fictions their "peculiar form," and explains his indebtedness to English literature and literary forms. Saito also discusses the psychological effect on Hawthorne of his tenure as American consul at Liverpool, which Saito sees as a source of Hawthorne's eventual disillusionment with both the English and the American social systems, a disillusionment that revealed itself in the material eventually collected in *Our Old Home*. Finally, Saito claims that Hawthorne owed the underlying structure of the four unfinished romances—in which English and American characteristics are compared and contrasted—to his English experiences.

Yoshitaka Aoyama, "Salvation Theme in *The Scarlet Letter*," *Studies in English Literature* 60 (1983): 245–60 (English summary in a 1984 English issue, 125–26). Aoyama argues that at least some of the ambiguities that swirl around the conclusion of *The Scarlet Letter* are illusory, and that, in fact, it is a salvation story, as a study of Hawthorne's use of typology in the description of the morphology of Dimmesdale's conversion reveals. On the wall of Dimmesdale's chamber hangs a tapestry depicting "the Scriptural story of David and Bathsheba, and Nathan the Prophet," and his conversion experience follows the morphology of David's conversion in the Bible, as suggested by Hawthorne's phrase "Thou art thyself the man!" This, of course, echoes the biblical line "Thou *art* the man." Hester's flaunting of the Scarlet Letter makes her symbolic of humanism and free will, but in the end she too is penitent, and the "one tombstone [that] served for both" is symbolic of the apocalyptic marriage that awaits them before the bar of final judgment.

Satoshi Okabe, "Hawthorne's Criticism of Margaret Fuller," *Tohoku Studies in American Literature*, no. 7 (1983) (English summary). Okabe contends that the severe criticism of Margaret Fuller that Hawthorne jotted down in his Italian notebook in 1858 was not unusual, but characteristic of his views on women and feminism as expressed elsewhere in his work. Okabe notes further that no evidence of a feud between the two authors, which might have made Hawthorne's outburst more understandable, is to be found in the letters and diaries of either, or in Fuller's comments on Hawthorne's works, but that Fuller's "lifelong ideal of self-culture" obviously conflicted with Hawthorne's attitudes about the proper role of women in Victorian society. Okabe then goes on to examine the parallels between Fuller and Zenobia in Hawthorne's *The Blithedale Romance*, arguing that Zenobia was "a new woman deeply colored with Fuller's characteristics," and that Hawthorne's explanation of the reasons for her tragic fate anticipates the form his criticism of Fuller would take in 1858.

Nobuyuki Hayashi, "Hawthorne and Stratford-on-Avon—Of His

'Recollections of a Gifted Woman,'" *Studies in English Language and Literature* 9 (1984): 86 (English summary of a publication of the English Language and Literary Society, Soka University). The "gifted woman" of Hawthorne's essay in *Our Old Home* was Delia Bacon, a "monomaniac" (as Hawthorne himself referred to her) possessed by the belief that the works attributed to Shakespeare had in fact been written by Lord Bacon. Hawthorne—then American consul at Liverpool—was sympathetic when she asked him for help in getting her book published, and even assisted her financially. Hayashi examines the "principle" that led Hawthorne to undertake such a "self-contradictory" action in light of the attitude toward Shakespeare that Hawthorne revealed in his work, and especially in his account of his visit to Stratford-on-Avon.

Takuo Miyake, "Narrative Discourse for Creating [the] Miraculous Lady and Butterfly—A Study of Hawthorne's Artist Tales," *Bulletin of the Faculty of Literature, Nara Women's University* (1984) (English summary). Miyake examines "The Prophetic Pictures," "Drowne's Wooden Image," and "The Artist of the Beautiful"—three tales that are very different, although in each an artist creates a miraculous work of art—and discusses each in terms of the type of artist presented, the relevant social and historical background, and the narrative method (or nature of the "discourse") employed.

Kazuko Takemura, "On 'Ethan Brand'—An Interpretation of Its Subtitle," *Studies in American Literature*, no. 21 (1984) (English summary, 97–98). Noting that "Ethan Brand" is subtitled "An Abortive Romance," Takemura sees the tale as abortive in the sense that the text, as we have it, contains allusions and references to events (Ethan Brand's quest for the "Unpardonable Sin," for example) that were described in chapters that no longer exist, or that were to have been described in chapters that had no existence except in Hawthorne's imagination. Takemura argues that there was a rationale for Hawthorne's deliberate adoption of an "abortive" form (beyond the Gothic or Romantic love of the fragment) in that it permitted him to avoid having to describe the impossible—the nature and depiction of the unpardonable sin itself. Detecting a shift from "restrained narrative style to fluent depiction," and a change in tone from "abstract" to "descriptive," Takemura also sees the story as being written during a transitional phase of Hawthorne's career, as he left short-story writing behind to turn to the production of romances.

Mamoru Tohtake, "Eros and Agape: A Note on 'Rappaccini's Daughter,'" *Journal of the English Institute of Tohoku Gakuin University,* no. 13 (1984): 27–47 (English summary, 75–76). Tohtake suggests that the "enigmatic ambiguity and deep-rooted complexity" of "Rappaccini's Daughter," a story that has long baffled its readers, are due in part to the fact that different sorts of love are at work in the story. Dr. Rappaccini, whose love for his daughter Beatrice is a "degraded, self-satisfying one," and Giovanni, whose love is innocent but immature and "cruelly selfish," are capable only of a diminished state of eros, and the story reaches its tragic conclusion because they are unable to share in or comprehend Beatrice's agape, or "heavenly and self-sacrificing" love.

Hiroko Washizu, "Re-Building a House: An Approach to *The House of the Seven Gables,*" *Studies in English Literature* (English summary in an English issue, 129–30). Washizu suggests that "moralistic" readings of *The House of the Seven Gables* fail to "provide a satisfactorily positive interpretation of the ending." In Hawthorne's preface, seen here as a work "about building a house," the "Author" (himself a fictional character) refers to the importance of mingling the two modes of romance and novel, and in the romance itself the relationship between the Maules and the Pyncheons represents this mingling, the romance mode (the Maules) being "suppressed" by the novel mode (the Pyncheons). The "Alice Pyncheon" chapter marks the inversion of this relationship, and also introduces the requisite "mingling" in the form of the marriage between Holgrave and Phoebe, necessary if the "[hi]story" of the house is to be completed. Thus the work as a whole has the structure of a nest of Chinese boxes: the characters, the author of the preface, and Hawthorne himself have all constructed houses—to which critic and reader, each rebuilding the house in his or her own way, add their own.

Fumio Ano, "Hawthorne's View of the Negro," *Tohoku Studies in American Literature,* no. 9 (1985): 65–66. Ano examines the picture that emerges when we assemble the various thoughts on African-Americans, slavery, and the Civil War that crop up from time to time—in more or less charged contexts—in various works by Hawthorne. Such references appear, for example, in *The American Magazine of Useful and Entertaining Knowledge,* which the youthful Hawthorne edited for a time in 1836; in the *Life of Franklin Pierce,* which he wrote when his former classmate and longtime friend became a candidate for the presidency; in the late sketch "Chiefly about War Matters"; and in a wartime letter to Harriet

Carte-de-visite of Nathaniel Hawthorne taken by Silsbee, Case, & Co. in 1861. The photograph was donated to the Peabody Essex Museum by Barbara L. Bacheler.

Beecher Stowe. Ano notes that Hawthorne was much less enthusiastic about the abolitionist movement than were such contemporaries as Thoreau and Emerson, and maintains that, even if Hawthorne was, as he himself said, "rather more of an abolitionist in feeling than in principle," he was willing to allow the continued existence of slavery if it meant that the Union could be preserved, assuming that when Divine Providence saw fit, slavery would "vanish like a dream." Hawthorne reveals a great deal to a modern reader when he admits to being repulsed by the "foppery of the race in our parts" (in the North, that is); he preferred what he insisted on seeing as the exuberant exoticism of southern Negroes who wore "such a crust of primeval simplicity" that they seemed "not altogether human, but perhaps quite as good," and whom he likened to "the fauns and rustic deities of olden times"—employing imagery, interestingly enough, that he had also used to characterize the initial impression that Donatello (childlike, unsophisticated, Italian, and Roman Catholic) makes upon the puritanical but more highly "cultured" Yankees in *The Marble Faun.*

Fumio Ano, "Hawthorne and Poison," *Rising Generation* 131 (1985): 117–19. Ano considers Jemshed A. Khan's hypothesis that in *The Scarlet Letter* Chillingworth had brought about the illness and eventual death of Dimmesdale by poisoning him with atropine, which Hawthorne knew of because he had read about deadly nightshade and henbane in a book on botany. Khan explains much of Dimmesdale's strange behavior as symptomatic of such poisoning—suggesting, for example, that Dimmesdale often puts his hand upon his heart because he is experiencing angina "exacerbated by atropine-induced tachycardia." Ano wonders, however, why Chillingworth—who, because he seeks revenge, wants to prolong Dimmesdale's torments as long as possible—should want to poison his victim. He notes, too, that Dimmesdale puts his hand over his heart before he has ever met Chillingworth, and that other "symptoms" of poisoning may be accounted for in other ways. Ano goes on, however, to summarize evidence that Hawthorne may have been as interested in poisons as he was in the "elixir of life." Suggesting that this interest was characteristic of writers who worked in the Gothic tradition, Ano cites as an example "The Poisoned Garden," in the writing of which the Russian decadent Fyodor Sologub was, as Patricia Pollock Brodsky has noted, heavily influenced by Hawthorne's "Rappaccini's Daughter"—a story saturated with poisonous influences, both physical and moral.

Mutsuo Fujisaki, "Ambiguity and Time: Hawthorne's Imagination," *Studies in English Language and Literature,* no. 35 (1985): 169 (English summary). Fujisaki discusses the function of Hawthorne's "ambiguity device" in "The Custom-House" and "The Haunted Mind," regarding it as "the essence of his creative imagination." He also argues that Hawthorne sees the past as repeating itself in the present, and reads "My Kinsman, Major Molineux" as a story in which the ambiguity devices (moonlight, dream imagery, and darkness) help to transform a historical event into a symbolic one possessed of multiple meanings—the tarring and feathering of Major Molineux on the eve of the American Revolution functioning as a reenactment of the ancient rituals relating to the crowning and deposition of the Scapegoat King.

Katsotoshi Hoshino, "'The Sibyl's Golden Bough': Hawthorne in *Clarel,*" *Nathaniel Hawthorne Society of Japan Newsletter,* no. 4 (1985): 5. Hoshino summarizes the evidence in favor of the assumption that the character "Vine" in Melville's *Clarel* is based on Hawthorne, and notes that, at the time Melville wrote this late work (1876), he no longer had hopes, as he himself put it, of "coming at his [Hawthorne's] mystery."

Noriaki Koyama, "Hawthorne's View of the American Revolution," *Chu-Shikoku Studies in American Literature,* no. 21 (June 1985): 34–47 (English summary, 46–47). Taken together, Koyama affirms, the Hawthornean tales that employ the American Revolution as the setting or subject tend to contradict each other, and so reveal the complexity of Hawthorne's attitudes toward this "historic event." Thus, there are "patriotic" stories such as "The Gray Champion," more skeptical ones (such as "Endicott and the Red Cross") that suggest that Hawthorne "was not satisfied with the complacent image of the Revolution prevalent in his days," darker ones such as "My Kinsman, Major Molineux," that reveal the "villainous actions of patriotic mobs," and ones such as "Old Esther Dudley" that are intended to arouse in the reader "strong sympathies for the defeated royalists." Hawthorne's Revolutionary War tales, then, reflect both his "sincere effort to grasp and represent the whole truth" of the complex issues and events involved and his "magnanimous view of man"—that is, his reluctance to condemn those who remained faithful to a mistaken cause.

Teruhiko Mukai, "Concord and the Wilderness: Emerson, Thoreau and Hawthorne," *Tohoku Studies in American Literature,* no. 9 (1985): 63 (English summary). Mukai maintains that Hawthorne created his own version of Concord—a solitary world of the imagination, a wilderness that at different times could symbolize America or the psyche—that contrasts with Emerson's Concord (a realm sublime and transcendental) and with Thoreau's (the center of a harmonious wilderness).

Satoshi Okabe, "An Interpretation of Miles Coverdale's Confession," *Tohoku Studies in American Literature,* no. 9 (1985). Okabe attempts to get at the "real intention and true meaning" of the celebrated confession at the end of *The Blithedale Romance* by examining Coverdale's "feelings of futility at the time of his 'meridian manhood.'" Okabe suggests that, because Coverdale views Zenobia as a "challenging riddle" while she attacks him for his inquisitiveness (reflecting Hawthorne's sense of the inherently guilty nature of his own creative process), their relationship is so fraught with conflict that Coverdale could never have become infatuated with her. The different attitude he manifests toward Priscilla, however, and her passivity, provide "evidence enough to make his confession coherent." Finally, Okabe argues that Coverdale's feelings of futility are born of the conflict between his desire to be an active participant in life and his tendency as an artist toward isolation, vicariousness, and idealism. Coverdale's confession, then, is intended as both "an ironic consummation of his futile life and a retribution for his egotism."

Mamoru Tohtake, "Dreams of Ascending and Fears of Falling: *The Marble Faun* and Italy," *Tohoku Studies in American Literature,* no. 9 (1985): 36–51 (English summary). Tohtake notes that, in Hawthorne's four completed romances, dynamic spatial images of upward and downward movement (reflecting the Christian view that God is above in heaven while Satan is below in hell) recur most frequently in *The Marble Faun,* where they play a significant role in the development of theme and characterization. They do so, he believes, because "the relics, pictures, statues, and legends Hawthorne encountered in Italy [seem] to have etched the images of vertical movement in his imagination." The structures involved include Hilda's tower, the catacomb of St. Calixtus, the chasm in the legend of Curtius, the treatise on Guido Reni's *Archangel Michael,* the Dome of St. Peter's, and Donatello's Owl-Tower.

Aoyama Yoshitaka, "Hawthorne and the Bible," *Nathaniel Hawthorne*

Society of Japan Newsletter, no. 4 (1985): 3–4. Aoyama expands on his earlier essay, emphasizing the need for further understanding of Hawthorne's indebtedness to the Bible by noting that Hawthorne echoed texts from Rev. 16:6 and Rev. 16:7 at crucial points in *The House of the Seven Gables,* laying the groundwork for the apocalyptic ending of the romance.

Hisao Inoue, "On Robin's Laughter in 'My Kinsman, Major Molineux,'" *Studies in American Literature,* no. 23 (1986) (English summary, 33–34). Inoue notes that, although there are a great many varying critical opinions as to the significance of Robin Molineux's laughter when he confronts his uncle at the conclusion of Hawthorne's story, all of them suggest, in effect, that he is laughing either at his kinsman or at himself. Inoue proposes, however, that the "shrewd" Robin is laughing at the mob that, having tarred and feathered Major Molineux, is parading him through the streets of Boston. The fact that Robin's shout is "the loudest there," then, does not signify his acquiescence in their act, or the dawning of a rueful self-awareness of his own folly, but his resistance to the multitude.

Keisuke Kawakubo, "Hawthorne's Agony: A Modern Meaning," *Nathaniel Hawthorne Society of Japan Newsletter,* no. 5 (1986): 2. In this meditation on the effect that Hawthorne's years in England and Europe might have had on his art and life, Kawakubo undertakes to show that, during Hawthorne's tenure as American consul at Liverpool, he lost more and more of his American perspective as he acclimated himself to English culture; that in Italy his inherited Calvinist sensibilities were further shaken by his encounters with "overwhelming cultural treasures and Catholicism"; and that the anxiety he felt was similar to that experienced by the Japanese scholar Mori Ogai, who, studying in Germany during the 1880s, found himself torn between the spiritual and ethical values of the West and those of traditional Japan. Although Ogai chose to return to Japan, Kawakubo informs us, his later years were tinged with "a sorrowful 'resignation.'"

Hideo Masuda, "The Interdisciplinary Approach and Its Relevance: The 'Atropine Poisoning' of Arthur Dimmesdale," *Nathaniel Hawthorne Society of Japan Newsletter,* no. 5 (1986): 1. Masuda joins Ano in viewing Khan's atropine hypothesis as ingenious but incorrect because it would conflict with Hawthorne's concept of sin and its effects. If Chillingworth were really poisoning Dimmesdale, the latter's psychological torment would become merely pathological suffering, and the episode as a whole would lose its significance as an indicator of the physical, psychological, and spiritual effects of guilt upon the sinner.

Hideo Masuda, "'Roger Malvin's Burial': Sin and Its Expiation in Hawthorne," *Hiroshima Studies in English Language and Literature,* no. 31 (1986): 39–48. "Roger Malvin's Burial" seems bewildering, Masuda argues, because it has been approached from psychological or theological perspectives that may be misleading. Masuda believes that Reuben Bourne's "self-interest and his dissimulation of the truth constitute sin as Nathaniel Hawthorne sees it," an observation that is illustrated with a number of examples of similar behavior found in other works by Hawthorne. "In Hawthorne's work," Masuda goes on to say, "the expiation of sin, when it is possible, is effected through penitence"—not merely through penance. This penitence, too, must be public in some sense, returning the sinner to his place in the midst of fallible humanity. Thus, the various psychoanalytic interpretations of the story tend to ignore the import of the final scene—in which Bourne kills his son—to the extent that they suggest that what he goes through is not penitence but "psychological catharsis." The story ends as it does, Masuda insists, because of divine intervention, "preordained" in order to make possible the remission of Bourne's sin. "What torments him," Masuda insists, "is not something that a psychoanalyst can take care of: despite the fact that it shows the author's penetrating insight into the abyss of man's psychology, this story is not a mere anticipation of what the psychologists were to formulate in later years for the subconscious." Hawthorne, he concludes, knew full well that "the consequences of sin can be more inexorable than one might wish they were."

Shinichiro Noriguchi, "Archetypal Symbolism in the Works of Nathaniel Hawthorne," *Fukuoka Women's Junior College Studies,* pt. 1, 32 (1986): 33–56; pt. 2, 33 (1987): 57–78. Noriguchi notes that certain symbols seem to have evoked "essentially the same responses" in all societies at all times, and proceeds to locate such archetypal symbols in Hawthorne's tales and romances. Part 1 discusses Hawthorne's use of the archetypes of the quest or journey, light and darkness, and the demonic or paradisal garden, while the presence in his work of archetypes relating to the scapegoat, the fall of man, and death and rebirth are discussed in part 2, which also contains a detailed analysis of archetypal imagery in *The Scarlet Letter,* "which is of special interest to Japanese students and is read widely."

Sachiko Saito, "Nathaniel Hawthorne: The Italian Years," *Hikaku Bungaka Journal of Comparative Literature* 29 (1986): 81–92 (English summary, 186). Saito avers that Hawthorne created a fairy land in which to situate his romances out of necessity, because "there was hardly any strange, antique, or pictorial enchantment in America." His interest in Italy and Italian culture seems to have developed after he met Sophia Peabody, and may be attributable to her influence. During the time he lived there, he found Italy to be a world in which past, present, and eternity were all "manifest and observable," and he found there, too, the requisite atmosphere and all the materials necessary for a romance, perhaps too readily at hand.

Kimiko Tokunaga, "Pearl's Function in *The Scarlet Letter,*" *Kyushu American Literature* 27 (1986): 1–12. Tokunaga gives attention to Pearl's "mysterious role" in *The Scarlet Letter,* examining her as a child of nature, as a mirror reflecting Hester, as a visible and invisible scarlet letter, and as an implier of facts.

Under the first heading, Tokunaga suggests that Pearl is portrayed ambiguously, since she functions both as child and as symbol. Hawthorne adopts a variety of ways to characterize her beauty—she is described as a wildflower, a princess, and so forth—and her presence is a "beam of light" that illuminates this "dark story." Full of vitality, she gives life to others. She is closely linked with the forest, an expression of nature, which although it is amoral, can become evil when man chooses to follow Satan instead of God. Neither the forest nor Pearl is subject to the law, human or divine: she is "free from the codes which society sets up to regulate social behavior," and becomes a symbol both of the grace of nature and of the grace of God. Born as an innocent in amoral nature, she nevertheless attains human sympathy and accepts her place in society, and as the "flower" of the story, she symbolizes a moral—"the stern teaching of being true."

Second, Hawthorne often suggests that character or mentality is betrayed by outward characteristics. Thus, the "exotic appearance" of Hester and Pearl symbolizes their "internal heretical richness." Hester's passion manifests itself as sin, but Pearl's becomes courage, pride, a scorn of falsehood, and the capacity for love, which Tokunaga sees as an indication that Hawthorne "tried to grow different kinds of flowers from the same soil of passion." Pearl's mental disorder, formed in the womb, mirrors Hester's "emotional disturbance and anguish," and Hester's belief that her child is possessed by an evil spirit is an obsession caused by her own sin—the dark side of her own heart being reflected in Pearl.

Third, Pearl is seen as a living symbol of Hester's adultery. She serves to connect Hester with heaven, but also, as the object of her affection, protects her from vicious temptations. Although at first Pearl causes Hester only pain, the latter comes to think that the purpose of this Divine Providence is one of "mercy and beneficence." The joy and sorrow caused by Pearl uplift Hester—her sinful passion becomes maternal love—and when, in the forest, Hester and Dimmesdale think to flee the consequences of their sin, Pearl's refusal to accept Hester's casting away of the Scarlet Letter manifests the voice of God. After Pearl washes off his kiss in the brook, Dimmesdale comes to realize that not Hester but only the grace of God can save him, and in the end, as Hawthorne has it, "Pearl's errand as a messenger of anguish was all fulfilled": she shows her parents "the right way through their anguish," acting as "a messenger who shows the way to heaven for both of her parents."

Finally, Tokunaga argues that although Pearl as a child is fey, and thus preternaturally aware of hidden truths, after she is "reconciled with her earthly father," she gains human sympathy and becomes completely human.

Tokunaga's conclusion is that because Pearl functions first and foremost as a messenger, she is "a symbol rather than a character." She has no true mental development, but "suddenly becomes realistic" after fulfilling her function as a symbolic scarlet letter. We ought not to look for psychological "reality," however, in a romance, in which, as Hawthorne notes, the writer can present "the truth of the human heart under circumstances of his own choosing." Ultimately Pearl is best seen as "the eternal beauty deep in the human heart," or at least as a "light of hope," since as an adult she resembles Hester's vision of the "angel and apostle of the coming revelation."

Mamoru Tohtake, "Uncertainty of Interpretation: 'The Birth-mark' as *Opera Aperta*," *Journal of the English Institute of Tohoku Gakuin University*, no. 15 (1986): 95–113. Tohtake contends that critics have been unable to reach a consensus as to how we should characterize Aylmer—as egotistical monster or noble seeker after truth—because "The Birthmark" is what Umberto Eco calls an *opera aperta,* a work that "delivers no definite message but discloses the . . . fact that our world is an enigma to be solved." The story, Tohtake believes, concerns itself with the relationship between man and nature, "an eternal aporia as old as history": because man is fallen, he cannot live in harmony with nature, but he also possesses the desire—and the ability—to "improve" it. Aylmer's attempt to eradicate Georgiana's birthmark is thus both "a blasphemous attempt at self-deification" and "a very noble act," and the uncertainty surrounding all critical attempts to decode the aporia reflects "the uncertainty of the situation in which we still find ourselves today" (with regard to our own sense of our relationship with nature).

Fumio Ano, "Hawthorne's View of England in 'Legends of the Province-House,'" *Bulletin of the College of General Education, Tohoku University,* no. 48 (1987): 81–98 (English summary, 99). Ano notes that the four stories that make up "Legends of the Province-House" were written as a series, and thus possess an organic unity first commented upon by Robert H. Fossum. Ano enlarges upon Fossum's insight by noting that the apparent glorification of the American cause in "Howe's Masquerade" and "Edward Randolph's Portrait" is ironic when viewed in light of the sympathy for England (and criticism of America) expressed in "Lady Eleanore's Mantle" and "Old Esther Dudley." Ano reads the "Legends" as a whole, then, as expressing a typically Hawthornean ambivalence (or pessimism) about the way Americans tend to interpret their own history.

Mutsuo Fujisaki, "From History to Legend: 'Alice Doane's Appeal' and 'Legends of the Province-House,'" *Studies in English Language and Literature,* no. 37 (1987): 115 (English summary). Fujisaki believes that the narrator of "Alice Doane's Appeal" calls up "the shadowy past"—not "empirical historical facts," but things excluded from history as "irrational"—in order to hold the attention of his audience in the present, and maintains that in Hawthorne's work the past is introduced into the present by means of legends, which possess their own circular structure rather than the linear or chronological structure of history. It was upon this basis that Hawthorne organized "Legends of the Province-House," in which he arranges four historical events in a circular pattern where multiple narrators, mirrors, portraits, and the Province-

House itself, with its winding staircase, mediate between the events themselves and the reader, thus facilitating the transmutation of history into legend.

Yoshio Isaka, "Fiction as a Whole," *Nathaniel Hawthorne Society of Japan Newsletter,* no. 6 (1987): 7–8. In a meditation on the sort of relationship one may have with the subject of one's research, Isaka draws upon charming personal experiences in Hawthorne country (on the last day of 1982, for example, he sat down on the steps of Salem City Hall, as "the Old Year" in Hawthorne's "The Sister Years" had done long before him). He concludes that the questions asked by those who seek to understand Hawthorne should concern how he lived, who surrounded him, what "the trend of [his] times" was, and how his imagination worked.

Mayumi Kurosaki, "Hawthorne's England, My England," *Nathaniel Hawthorne Society of Japan Newsletter,* no. 6 (1987): 8–9. In 1982, Kurosaki had an opportunity to visit Hawthorne's "Old Home," and, possessed of "little money and little time," but with "deep emotion," followed the ancestral footsteps through Liverpool, Stratford-on-Avon, Old Boston, Oxford, London, and elsewhere. Hawthorne, he notes, must have been "quite a strong walker. I wore out two pairs of shoes in two months." He was surprised and saddened, however, by the lack of interest in Hawthorne: "During my stay in England, I met no Englishman, excepting professors of literature, who knew the American writer."

Kazuko Takemura, "Dreaming in Hawthorne and Borges," *Nathaniel Hawthorne Society of Japan Newsletter,* no. 6 (1987): 3–4. Takemura uses comments from Borges's essay on Hawthorne to make the point that for both writers the function of the heart was to dream, thus creating and actualizing the world itself.

Koki Sato, "Hawthorne Accepted at Colleges and Universities," *Nathaniel Hawthorne Society of Japan Newsletter,* no. 6 (1987): 1–3. Sato notes that, during the Meiji era (1868–1912), various stories and sketches by Hawthorne found their way into the English-language textbooks and "cram-books" used by Japanese students. Although most translators tried to avoid works with "Christian themes dealing with 'sin,'" even such tales as "The Minister's Black Veil," and "Fancy's Show Box" ("which have long been liked by the Japanese people") were most often treated as juvenile literature. By the late nineteenth century, biographical and critical material on Hawthorne was also appearing in various textbooks used at Tokyo University and elsewhere. Most interestingly, Sato reveals that the first college and university lectures on Hawthorne and his works were not given until after the commencement of the Taisho era (1912–26), and provides a list of such lectures presented between 1920 and 1959. "Today so many papers are read and so many essays are written on Hawthorne that we cannot keep up with all of them."

Kumiko Mukai, "The Ending of *The House of the Seven Gables:* A Dual Aspect," *Kyushu American Literature* 29 (1988): 41–49. Noting that the "happy ending" of *The House of the Seven Gables* seems to conflict with its ostensible "moral," Mukai attempts to make sense of the work in light of Hawthorne's views on romance as he expressed them in his preface. The structure of the work, Mukai suggests, mingles the "Imaginary" with the "Actual," and the marvelous with at least two sorts of "realism"—one that attempts "the faithful delineation of life," and another that is at least in part autobiographical. Although one group of critics has suggested that the ending cannot be seen as "realistic" in any meaningful sense while another insists that the ending is ironic, and that a darker reality lurks behind the sunny surface, Mukai believes that the fact that the final paragraph seems both optimistic (in its reference to Maule's well) and foreboding (in its reference to the Pyncheon elm) implies something about Hawthorne's abiding sense of the essential duality of things. He could not, that is, ignore his sense that life (as he himself put it in *The House of the Seven Gables*) is made up of both "marble" and "mud" without failing in his attempt to obey the truth of his heart.

Satoshi Okabe, "The Use of Irony in Hawthorne's Four Short Stories," *Bulletin of Tohoku Institute of Technology*, no. 8 (1988): 19 (English summary). Okabe examines Hawthorne's use of irony in "The Ambitious Guest," "The Minister's Black Veil," "The Birth-mark," and "The Artist of the Beautiful," concluding that it is "most characteristic and effective as a vehicle of the multiple complexity of meaning when it is concerned with the concealed or unconscious workings of the human heart." It was through his use of irony, Okabe believes, that Hawthorne was able to express his truths despite the conflict between his "puritan moral bias" and his romantic idealism.

Jūkichi Suzuki, "Hawthorne and Keats," *Nathaniel Hawthorne Society of Japan Newsletter*, no. 7 (1988): 1–2. Suzuki sees similarities in the creative processes of Keats and Hawthorne, identifying the "Negative Capability" of the former with what Hawthorne (in "The Haunted Mind") referred to as "passive sensibility." The fact that both men worked by passively recording images from the unconscious mind predisposed them toward ambiguity and to imagery relating to caves, tombs, and dungeons. Noting that the development of "Rappaccini's Daughter" was influenced by Hawthorne's reading of Keats's "Lamia," Suzuki goes on to describe some of the probable sources of Hawthorne's information on Keats's life and works.

Shigeru Suzuki, "'An Ascending Spiral Curve': The Cycle of Integration, Isolation, and Re-Integration in Hawthorne," *University of Saga Studies in English* 16 (1988): 1–43. Suzuki notes that Hawthorne worked within a tradition (inherited from Cooper, who had it from Scott) that recognized two sorts of women: "fair ladies" (tending toward blondness, not particularly beautiful, or sexually attractive, but good, innocent, and associated with sunshine, hearth, and home), and "dark ladies" (creatures of night, exotic, voluptuous, but possessed of guilty secrets, and thus dangerous both sexually and morally). The fair women, angelic and salvific, rescue male protagonists who might otherwise go astray, or redeem those who have already done so, while the dark ones either run away themselves, or induce males to do so. (In this regard, as in so many others, the ambiguous Beatrice Rappaccini seems a sort of hybrid—as is Pearl, to a lesser extent, in *The Scarlet Letter.*) The fair women urge male characters to confess their sins and redeem themselves, while men who fall under the malign influence of the dark ladies torment themselves with guilty secrets. Although some (Westervelt and Judge Pyncheon, for example) manage to present a falsely attractive exterior to the world, Hawthorne's villains—whether male or female—tend to be old, skinny, and ugly, and they function much as the dark ladies do: keepers of secrets who lure their victims away from ordinary walks of life, torture them in either a physical or a psychological sense, and ultimately destroy them. Unlike the dark ladies, however, who tend to act impulsively, under the influence of passion, the villains are cold and calculating, and intend from the start to destroy their victims. Sometimes (as in "Rappaccini's Daughter") a villain uses a dark lady as bait to lead his chosen victim astray.

All of these characters—ladies both fair and dark, villains, and victims—appear in Hawthorne's four major romances, which share certain structural tendencies. Protagonists appear to have become an integral part of a society, but dark ladies controlled by villains lead them astray. Fallen protagonists then hide secrets that cause them to be isolated from society, but fair ladies urge them to unburden themselves. The protagonists waver, but in the end place themselves in the hands of the fair ladies, and are thus reintegrated into society. Suzuki then proceeds with a detailed examination of the ways in which this basic pattern of "integration, isolation, and re-integration," reinforced by imagery that emphasizes light, then darkness, then light again, is developed in both *The Scarlet Letter* and *The House of the Seven Gables,* showing that the characters in Hawthorne's work who grow and mature as human beings do so by following what Hawthorne himself referred to as an "ascending spiral curve," moving from an apparent "integration" through a period of isolation and on to a genuine integration with society.

Mutsuo Fujisaki, "*The House of the Seven Gables:* Romance and Reality," *Studies in English Language and Literature,* no. 39 (1989): 141 (English summary). Fujisaki suggests that the writing of *The House of the Seven Gables* required "more care and thought," as Hawthorne himself put it, than the writing of *The Scarlet Letter* had done because he was consciously attempting to imbue the former with the "sunshine" that the latter so conspicuously lacked. By "sunshine," Fujisaki believes, Hawthorne meant "realistic light sketches of the present ordinary life" would have more appeal for the reader of his day. Hawthorne's skill, however, lay in his ability to deal with the past, "which could be reduced to a single packed dramatic image in the form of a romance," and his attempt to mingle past gloom and present sunshine weakened the structure of *The House of the Seven Gables.* Hawthorne's attempt to combine past and present, however, implies that a shift from romanticism to realism was already underway in American literature.

Kumiko Mukai, "Hawthorne's Artists 'Reading the Heart,'" *Kyushu American Literature* 30 (1989): 41–48. Regarding Hawthorne as a great artist, possessed of "deep humanity," Kumiko Mukai looks at heart imagery in various works and examines the ways in which Hawthorne's "artists"—including scientists, scholars, doctors, and so on—read hearts as part of their artistic and personal lives. She finds that, although Hawthorne's early tales may be discussed in terms of F. O. Matthiessen's "Head-Heart Psychology," heart-reading in Hawthorne's mature novels becomes more ambiguous and more complex. Mukai's study focuses on Roger Chillingworth of *The Scarlet Letter,* Holgrave of *The House of the Seven Gables,* and Miles Coverdale of *The Blithedale Romance.* The egoistic Chillingworth's reading of Hester's heart and then Dimmesdale's is an unpardonable sin because he does it in order to seek revenge. Holgrave's "reverence for another's individuality" helps him to avoid a similar fate. Coverdale's reading of Zenobia's heart reveals that she has more "heart" than he had assumed, and his own admission that he loves Priscilla reveals that he is not the cold egoist he has seemed. Mukai concludes that, although the ideal person should balance both "head" and "heart," "Hawthorne does not always regard extremely one-sided people as monomaniacs, nor does he reject them cold-heartedly." She quotes various critics (Mark Van Doren on Hawthorne's fear of his own powers of insight and analysis, and Nina Baym on the "intellectual sinners" who are in fact motivated by passion) in order to make the point that our appreciation of Hawthorne's "sympathetic expression of character" enables us to realize his "deep humanity." Her notes cite F. O. Matthiessen, Hubert H. Hoeltje, Randall Stewart, Edward Wagenknecht, Nina Baym, Marvin Laser, Donald A. Ringe, and Mark Van Doren—most of the critical material dating from 1941 to 1967.

Satoshi Okabe, "Beatrice Cenci: A Comparative Study of Hawthorne and Shelley," *Bulletin of Tohoku Institute of Technology,* no. 9 (1989) (English summary). Commenting that both Shelley and Hawthorne were deeply interested in the story of Beatrice Cenci, Okabe claims that faint traces of Shelley's influence can be detected in the otherwise "characteristic" treatment of the Cenci material in Hawthorne's *The Marble Faun.*

Shinji Takuwa, "Imagination of Poe and Hawthorne," *Nathaniel Hawthorne Society of Japan Newsletter,* no. 8 (1989): 1. This essay was based on Lafcadio Hearn's lecture on "American Literature," given at Tokyo Imperial University in 1898. Hearn concluded that, although both authors had powerful imaginations, they differed in that Poe was "strikingly deficient" in the moral sense, which Hawthorne possessed to an excessive degree.

Fumio Ano, "'The Great Stone Face': Another Reading," *Nathaniel Hawthorne Society of Japan Newsletter,* no. 9 (1990): 2–3. Ano asserts that Ernest's quest for the Great Stone Face is the counterpart of Hawthorne's own lifelong quest for the father whom he had lost in childhood. The false counterparts of the Great Stone Face recall Robert Manning, and Gathergold's mansion is a version of "Manning's Folly," as the Manning house in Raymond, Maine, was called when it was constructed in 1810. Ernest's reluctance to admit that he himself is the image of the Great Stone Face suggests that Hawthorne never expected to find a father figure, and that he was reluctant to assume the role of father in his own right.

Muneharu Kitagaki, "English Periodical Essays and Hawthorne: A Few Suggestions," *Nathaniel Hawthorne Society of Japan Newsletter,* no. 9 (1990): 1–2. Kitagaki remarks upon Hawthorne's love of eighteenth-century English literature, and particularly on his interest in the work of Addison and Johnson, which certainly influenced the development of his prose style.

Suzuko Shindo, "The Black Man in *The Scarlet Letter,*" *Studies in American Literature,* no. 27 (1990): 1–16. Shindo notes that Hawthorne's works were born from his "night thoughts," which he sought out because he sensed that the genesis of all things and the source of all human consciousness lay in primal night, in the darkness, never conquered by light or reason, that exerts its authority "in the form of the irrational." In the Christian world, according to Shindo, this power is traditionally embodied in the Black Man whom the Puritans in particular associated with Satan and witchcraft. Roger Chillingworth becomes more and more like the Black Man of European and American tradition as he torments Arthur Dimmesdale in *The Scarlet Letter.* Chillingworth plays the role of "the Satan of the Book of Job," at which Hawthorne hints when he notes that "This diabolical agent had the Divine permission, for a reason [*sic*], to burrow into the clergyman's intimacy, and plot against his soul." Like Job, then, the minister overcomes Satan in the end by refusing to forsake God. Chillingworth's wife, Hester, has also tempted Dimmesdale, and the Puritans therefore view her as an emissary of Satan, but Shindo, accepting Hawthorne's "dark necessity" as the force motivating all three characters, sees irony in the fact that, in the very act of persecuting Hester, her tormenters themselves succumb to the temptations of the same Black Man whom they profess to abhor.

Masahiko Narita, "The Semiotic Arcadia: Hawthorne's *The Blithedale Romance,*" *Studies in American Literature,* no. 28 (1991): 1–17. Although *The Blithedale Romance* can be read as psychological autobiography, Narita informs us, it also contains an "elaborate subtext about the problem of literary creation," and through the persona of Miles Coverdale, Hawthorne reveals more about the dilemma in which he found himself as a writer of romances than he did anywhere else in his work. During the period from 1850 to 1852, Narita believes, Hawthorne shifted from allegory to romance because he found it increasingly necessary to express emotions that could not be confined within a "conventional literary framework." He was more and more tempted, that is, to "confront his own deeper self," and turned to the romance because it embodied a socially "radical" discourse that derived its power from the subconscious. In *The Blithedale Romance,* Narita believes, Hawthorne produced "a faithful record of his encounter with this great psychic source" of material that undermined or threatened the established social order. Narita invokes both Michael Davitt Bell's comments on the fundamentally revolutionary (or at least antisocial) nature of the romance itself and Julia Kristeva's belief in the close connection between "revolutionary literary expression and female sexual drives" in order to make the point that Blithedale is a "semiotized" Arcadia, and that the minor poet Coverdale desires to become "a true Kristevan poet." Coverdale's aim as a poet is to achieve greatness by recovering "the original picturesqueness of language," something that he intends to accomplish by "attuning" his work to "the rhythm of nature." "Nature," however, which is the artist's source of creativity, is not merely something external, but also something internal, something within the psyche—and here it is also seen as something feminine. Coverdale's womb-like "leafy cave" in the trees, for example, where the inner and outer natures overlap, is a place where he hopes to be imbued with and revitalized by "female sexual drives." Zenobia fascinates him (*contra* Millicent Bell, Nina Baym, and Leland S. Person, Jr.) because she is female power incarnate, and Coverdale remains at Blithedale itself because it is a sphere "permeated by" her feminine energy.

Such a source of energy is crucial to Coverdale's creativity, Narita explains, because of the distinction (expressed here in Kristevan terms, although it is pointed out that she had been anticipated by earlier artists, including Wordsworth and Margaret Fuller) between two modalities: the symbolic (from the father, the signifying process governing our daily verbal activity) and the semiotic (from the mother, a process full of instinctive drives and forces originally pre-Oedipal in nature). If poetic language becomes vitiated, the semiotic system can regenerate it, but only if the poet returns to the (incestuous) state of a pre-Oedipal infant embraced by his mother. Hence, as Kristeva has it, "poetic language is linked with 'evil.'" If Zenobia embodies the semiotic process, Westervelt (who in his "aggressiveness, masculine power, and wickedness" comes to disrupt the "semiotic Arcadia" of Blithedale) embodies the symbolic one, and the inability of men and women to interact harmoniously—emphasized by the gradual reclaiming of Blithedale itself by "the male-dominated power structure" of nineteenth-century America that the Blithedalers had rejected in the first place—betrays not only Hawthorne's sense that the semiotic system cannot exist by itself, but also his reluctance to devote himself entirely to "radical language."

To Narita, then, *The Blithedale Romance* is a "faithful dramatization" of what occurred in Hawthorne's own psyche when he descended into the "Blithedale realm within his own soul" in an attempt to express his own repressed passions and emotions. After the experiment, like Coverdale, Hawthorne returned in the end to "the conventional verbal system and the world of daily life"—at least until, some years later, he undertook *The Marble Faun.*

Kazuko Takemura, "A Drama of Relativity—One Representation of 'Historicality' in *The Blithedale Romance*," *Bulletin of the Faculty of Literature, Seikei University,* no. 26 (1991): 275–90. Adopting a deconstructive mode, Takemura first discusses the role played by Miles Coverdale (who functions as the chorus might have done in a classical play) in a theatrical Blithedale located midway between the real world and Hawthorne's fairyland. Takemura then goes on to examine "the relationship between romance, novel, and history" in the work, asserting that Hawthorne's narrative technique (one of several "measures for mystification") leads the reader back and forth between two "kinds of experience of time," mingling time past ("the retrospective time") and time present ("the successive time") in order to reveal (but only gradually, and partially, as through a veil) something of both the history and the future of each of the characters. The essay concludes with the view that Hawthorne's romance may be regarded as a representation of the "ardent yearnings" (not merely for a utopian society but for "perfect comprehension of human relationships or human society") that Takemura identifies with Heidegger's concept of "historicality," as defined in *Time and Being.*

The methodologies employed in the essays summarized above tend to be virtually identical with those recently in vogue in the United States; thus, one encounters various kinds of post-structuralist criticism, gender studies, linguistic analyses, legal/social studies, and so on. In Japan too, however, the emphasis may be shifting—as it seems to be doing in the United States—from theory to context. Historicism of one sort or another has long been popular (even dominant) in Japan, and many articles are devoted to explanations of matters that—readily comprehensible though they might have been to an American reader in Hawthorne's day—have become less and less accessible with the passing of time. Kazuko Takemura has recently commented on the return to historicism in his essay on the "Flowering of Hawthorne Criticism," in which he reviews American Hawthorne criticism produced during 1991, seeing a "return to history" in articles devoted to a "theoretical analysis of Hawthorne's historicity" or to a "sociological investigation of his texts and contexts" and a correspondingly strong emphasis on the exploration of the "complex interactions between a literary text and its political, social, and economic context."[15]

As a final note, I wish to leave the reader with a remark proffered by Shinichiro Noriguchi in the essay "Archetypal Symbolism in the Works of Nathaniel Hawthorne" to which I have already had occasion to refer. Noriguchi admits to being "challenged and frustrated" by the ambiguities he has encountered in Hawthorne's work—a condition with which all Hawthornians are certainly familiar. He leaves his readers, however, with the following bit of advice, which nicely sums up, I think, the attitude toward Hawthorne's work held by many Japanese scholars: "One who walks with Hawthorne should have abundant time and energy. In addition, a small lantern should be carried, for the way is not smooth and sometimes passes into a dark maze, but the scenery often presents infinite interest and colorful impression."[16]

15. Kazuko Takemura, "Flowering of Hawthorne Criticism," *Bulletin of the Nathaniel Hawthorne Society of Japan,* no. 10 (15 December 1991): 6–7.

16. Shinichiro Noriguchi, "Archetypal Symbolism," 76.

❁

DAVID SWAN

A FANTASY

WE CAN BE but partially acquainted even with events which actually influence our course through life, and our final destiny. There are innumerable other events, if such they may be called, which come close upon us, yet pass away without actual results, or even betraying their near approach, by the reflection of any light or shadow across our minds. Could we know all the vicissitudes of our fortunes, life would be too full of hope and fear, exultation or disappointment, to afford us a single hour of true serenity. This idea may be illustrated by a page from the secret history of David Swan.

We have nothing to do with David, until we find him, at the age of twenty, on the high road from his native place to the city of Boston, where his uncle, a small dealer in the grocery line, was to take him behind the counter. Be it enough to say, that he was a native of New Hampshire, born of respectable parents, and had received an ordinary school education, with a classic finish by a year at Gilmanton academy. After journeying on foot, from sunrise till nearly noon of a summer's day, his weariness and the increasing heat determined him to sit down in the first convenient shade, and await the coming up of the stage coach. As if planted on purpose for him, there soon appeared a little tuft of maples, with a delightful recess in the midst, and such a fresh bubbling spring, that it seemed never to have sparkled for any wayfarer but David Swan. Virgin or not, he kissed it with his thirsty lips, and then flung himself along the brink, pillowing his head upon some shirts and a pair of pantaloons, tied up in a striped cotton handkerchief. The sunbeams could not reach him; the dust did not yet rise from the road, after the heavy rain of yesterday; and his grassy lair suited the young man better than a bed of down. The spring murmured drowsily beside him; the branches waved dreamily across the blue sky, overhead; and a deep sleep, perchance hiding dreams within its depths, fell upon David Swan. But we are to relate events which he did not dream of.

While he lay sound asleep in the shade, other people were wide awake, and passed to and fro, a-foot, on horseback, and in all sorts of vehicles, along the sunny road by his bed-chamber. Some looked neither to the right hand nor to the left, and knew not that he was there; some merely glanced that way, without admitting the slumberer among their busy thoughts; some laughed to see how soundly he slept; and several, whose hearts were brimming full of scorn, ejected their venomous superfluity on David Swan. A middle aged widow, when nobody else was near, thrust her head a little way into the recess, and vowed that the young fellow looked charming in his sleep. A temperance lecturer saw him, and wrought poor David into the texture of his evening's discourse, as an awful instance of dead drunkenness by the road-side. But, censure, praise, merriment, scorn, and indifference, were all one, or rather all nothing, to David Swan.

He had slept only a few moments, when a brown carriage, drawn by a handsome pair of horses, bowled easily along, and was brought to a stand-still, nearly in front of David's resting place. A linch pin had fallen out, and permitted one of the wheels to slide off. The damage was slight, and occasioned merely a momentary alarm to an elderly merchant and his wife, who were returning to Boston in the carriage. While the coachman and a servant were replacing the wheel, the lady and gentleman sheltered themselves beneath the maple trees, and there espied the bubbling fountain, and David Swan asleep beside it. Impressed with the awe which the humblest sleeper usually sheds around him, the merchant trod as lightly as the gout would allow; and his spouse took good heed not to rustle her silk gown, lest David should start up, all of a sudden.

'How soundly he sleeps!' whispered the old gentleman. 'From what a depth he draws that easy breath! Such sleep as that, brought on without an opiate, would be worth more to me than half my income; for it would suppose health, and an untroubled mind.'

'And youth, besides,' said the lady. 'Healthy and quiet age does not sleep thus. Our slumber is no more like his, than our wakefulness.'

The longer they looked, the more did this elderly couple feel interested in the unknown youth, to whom the way side and the maple shade were as a secret chamber, with the rich gloom of damask curtains brooding over him. Perceiving that a stray sunbeam glimmered down upon his face, the lady contrived to twist a branch aside, so as to intercept it. And having done this little act of kindness, she began to feel like a mother to him.

'Providence seems to have laid him here,' whispered she to her husband, 'and to have brought us hither to find him, after our disappointment in our cousin's son. Methinks I can see a likeness to our departed Henry. Shall we waken him?'

'To what purpose?' said the merchant, hesitating. 'We know nothing of the youth's character.'

'That open countenance!' replied his wife, in the same hushed voice, yet earnestly. 'This innocent sleep!'

While these whispers were passing, the sleeper's heart did not throb, nor his breath become agitated, nor his features betray the least token of interest.—Yet Fortune was bending over him, just ready to let fall a burthen of gold. The old merchant had lost his only son, and had no heir to his wealth, except a distant relative, with whose conduct he was dissatisfied. In such cases, people sometimes do stranger things than to act the magician, and awaken a young man to splendor, who fell asleep in poverty.

'Shall we not waken him?' repeated the lady, persuasively.

'The coach is ready, Sir,' said the servant, behind.

The old couple started, reddened, and hurried away, mutually wondering, that they should ever have dreamed of doing any thing so very ridiculous. The merchant threw himself back in the carriage, and occupied his mind with the plan of a magnificent asylum for unfortunate men of business. Meanwhile, David Swan enjoyed his nap.

The carriage could not have gone above a mile or two, when a pretty young girl came along, with a tripping pace, which shewed precisely how her little heart was dancing in her bosom. Perhaps it was this merry kind of motion that caused—is there any harm in saying it?—her garter to slip its knot. Conscious that the silken girth, if silk it were, was relaxing its hold, she turned aside into the shelter of the maple trees, and there found a young man asleep by the spring! Blushing, as red as any rose, that she should have intruded into a gentleman's bed-chamber, and for such a purpose too, she was about to make her escape on tiptoe. But, there was peril near the sleeper. A monster of a bee had been wandering overhead—buzz, buzz, buzz—now among the leaves, now flashing through the strips of sunshine, and now lost in the dark shade, till finally he appeared to be settling on the eyelid of David Swan. The sting of a bee is sometimes deadly. As freehearted as she was innocent, the girl attacked the intruder with her handkerchief, brushed him soundly, and drove him from beneath the maple shade. How sweet a picture! This good deed accomplished, with quickened breath, and a deeper blush, she stole a glance at the youthful stranger, for whom she had been battling with a dragon in the air.

'He is handsome!' thought she, and blushed redder yet.

How could it be that no dream of bliss grew so strong within him, that, shattered by its very strength, it should part asunder, and allow him to perceive the girl among its phantoms? Why, at least, did no smile of welcome brighten upon his face? She was come, the maid whose soul, according to the old and beautiful idea, had been severed from his own, and whom, in all his vague but passionate desires, he yearned to meet. Her, only, could he love with a perfect love—him, only, could she receive into the depths of her heart—and now her image was faintly blushing in the fountain, by his side; should it pass away, its happy lustre would never gleam upon his life again.

'How sound he sleeps!' murmured the girl.

She departed, but did not trip along the road so lightly as when she came.

Now, this girl's father was a thriving country merchant in the neighbourhood, and happened, at that identical time, to be looking out for just such a young man as David Swan. Had David formed a way side acquaintance with the daughter, he would have become the father's clerk, and all else in natural succession. So here, again, had good fortune—the best of fortunes—stolen so near, that her garments brushed against him; and he knew nothing of the matter.

The girl was hardly out of sight, when two men turned aside beneath the maple shade. Both had dark faces, set off by cloth caps, which were drawn down aslant over their brows. Their dresses were shabby, yet had a certain smartness. These were a couple of rascals, who got their living by whatever the devil sent them, and now, in the interim of other business, had staked the joint profits of their next piece of villany on a game of cards, which was to have been decided here under the trees. But, finding David asleep by the spring, one of the rogues whispered to his fellow,

'Hist!—Do you see that bundle under his head?'

The other villain nodded, winked, and leered.

'I'll bet you a horn of brandy,' said the first, 'that the chap has either a pocket book, or a snug little hoard of small change, stowed away amongst his shirts. And if not there, we shall find it in his pantaloons' pocket.'

'But how if he wakes?' said the other.

His companion thrust aside his waistcoat, pointed to the handle of a dirk, and nodded.

'So be it!' muttered the second villain.

They approached the unconscious David, and, while one pointed the dagger towards his heart, the other began to search the bundle beneath his head. Their two faces, grim, wrinkled, and ghastly with guilt and fear, bent over their victim, looking horrible enough to be mistaken for fiends, should he suddenly awake. Nay, had the villains glanced aside into the spring, even they would hardly have known themselves, as reflected there. But David Swan had never worn a more tranquil aspect, even when asleep on his mother's breast.

'I must take away the bundle,' whispered one.

'If he stirs, I'll strike,' muttered the other.

But, at this moment, a dog, scenting along the ground, came in beneath the maple trees, and gazed alternately at each of these wicked men, and then at the quiet sleeper. He then lapped out of the fountain.

'Pshaw!' said one villain. 'We can do nothing now. The dog's master must be close behind.'

'Let's take a drink, and be off,' said the other.

The man, with the dagger, thrust back the weapon into his bosom, and drew forth a pocket pistol, but not of that kind which kills by a single discharge. It was a flask of liquor, with a block tin tumbler screwed upon the mouth. Each drank a comfortable dram, and left the spot, with so many jests, and such laughter at their unaccomplished wickedness, that they might be said to have gone on their way rejoicing. In a few hours, they had forgotten the whole affair, nor once imagined that the recording angel had written down the crime of murder against their souls, in letters as durable as eternity. As for David Swan, he still slept quietly, neither conscious of the shadow of death when it hung over him, nor of the glow of renewed life, when that shadow was withdrawn.

He slept, but no longer so quietly as at first. An hour's repose had snatched, from his elastic frame, the weariness with which many hours of toil had burthened it. Now, he stirred—now, moved his lips, without a sound—now, talked, in an inward tone, to the noon-day spectres of his dream. But a noise of wheels came rattling louder and louder along the road, until it dashed through the dispersing mist of David's slumber—and there was the stage coach. He started up, with all his ideas about him.

'Halloo, driver!—Take a passenger?' shouted he.

'Room on top!' answered the driver.

Up mounted David, and bowled away merrily towards Boston, without so much as a parting glance at that fountain of dreamlike vicissitude. He knew not that a phantom of Wealth had thrown a golden hue upon its waters—nor that one of Love had sighed softly to their murmur—nor that one of Death had threatened to crimson them with his blood—all, in the brief hour since he lay down to sleep. Sleeping or waking, we hear not the airy footsteps of the strange things that almost happen. Does it not argue a superintending Providence, that, while viewless and unexpected events thrust themselves continually athwart our path, there should still be regularity enough, in mortal life, to render foresight even partially available?

❀

FANCY'S SHOW BOX

A MORALITY

WHAT is Guilt? A stain upon the soul. And it is a point of vast interest, whether the soul may contract such stains, in all their depth and flagrancy, from deeds which may have been plotted and resolved upon, but which, physically, have never had existence. Must the fleshly hand, and visible frame of man, set its seal to the evil designs of the soul, in order to give them their entire validity against the sinner? Or, while none but crimes perpetrated are cognizable before an earthly tribunal, will guilty thoughts—of which guilty deeds are no more than shadows—will these draw down the full weight of a condemning sentence, in the supreme court of eternity? In the solitude of a midnight chamber, or in a desert, afar from men, or in a church, while the body is kneeling, the soul may pollute itself even with those crimes, which we are accustomed to deem altogether carnal. If this be true, it is a fearful truth.

Let us illustrate the subject by an imaginary example. A venerable gentleman, one Mr. Smith, who had long been regarded as a pattern of moral excellence, was warming his aged blood with a glass or two of generous wine. His children

The established text of this short story is reprinted with the permission of the editors of *Twice-told Tales*, volume nine of the Centenary Edition of the Works of Nathaniel Hawthorne published by the Ohio State University Center for Textual Studies (Columbus: Ohio State University Press, © 1974).

being gone forth about their worldly business, and his grand-children at school, he sat alone, in a deep, luxurious arm-chair, with his feet beneath a richly carved mahogany table. Some old people have a dread of solitude, and when better company may not be had, rejoice even to hear the quiet breathing of a babe, asleep upon the carpet. But Mr. Smith, whose silver hair was the bright symbol of a life unstained, except by such spots as are inseparable from human nature, he had no need of a babe to protect him by its purity, nor of a grown person, to stand between him and his own soul. Nevertheless, either Manhood must converse with Age, or Womanhood must soothe him with gentle cares, or Infancy must sport around his chair, or his thoughts will stray into the misty region of the past, and the old man be chill and sad. Wine will not always cheer him. Such might have been the case with Mr. Smith, when, through the brilliant medium of his glass of old Madeira, he beheld three figures entering the room. These were Fancy, who had assumed the garb and aspect of an itinerant showman, with a box of pictures on her back; and Memory, in the likeness of a clerk, with a pen behind her ear, an ink-horn at her button-hole, and a huge manuscript volume beneath her arm; and lastly, behind the other two, a person shrouded in a dusky mantle, which concealed both face and form. But Mr. Smith had a shrewd idea that it was Conscience.

How kind of Fancy, Memory, and Conscience, to visit the old gentleman, just as he was beginning to imagine that the wine had neither so bright a sparkle, nor so excellent a flavor, as when himself and the liquor were less aged! Through the dim length of the apartment, where crimson curtains muffled the glare of sunshine, and created a rich obscurity, the three guests drew near the silver-haired old man. Memory, with a finger between the leaves of her huge volume, placed herself at his right hand. Conscience, with her face still hidden in the dusky mantle, took her station on the left, so as to be next his heart; while Fancy set down her picture-box upon the table, with the magnifying glass convenient to his eye. We can sketch merely the outlines of two or three, out of the many pictures, which, at the pulling of a string, successively peopled the box with the semblances of living scenes.

One was a moonlight picture; in the back-ground, a lowly dwelling; and in front, partly shadowed by a tree, yet besprinkled with flakes of radiance, two youthful figures, male and female. The young man stood with folded arms, a haughty smile upon his lip, and a gleam of triumph in his eye, as he glanced downward at the kneeling girl. She was almost prostrate at his feet, evidently sinking under a weight of shame and anguish, which hardly allowed her to lift her clasped hands in supplication. Her eyes she could not lift. But neither her agony, nor the lovely features on which it was depicted, nor the slender grace of the form which it convulsed, appeared to soften the obduracy of the young man. He was the personification of triumphant scorn. Now, strange to say, as old Mr. Smith peeped through the mangifying glass, which made the objects start out from the canvass with magical deception, he began to recognize the farm-house, the tree, and both the figures of the picture. The young man, in times long past, had often met his gaze within the looking-glass; the girl was the very image of his first love—his cottage-love—his Martha Burroughs! Mr. Smith was scandalized. 'Oh, vile and slanderous picture!' he exclaims. 'When have I triumphed over ruined innocence? Was not Martha wedded, in her teens, to David Tomkins, who won her girlish love, and long enjoyed her affection as a wife? And ever since his death, she has lived a reputable widow!' Meantime, Memory was turning over the leaves of her volume, rustling them to and fro with uncertain fingers, until, among the earlier pages, she found one which had reference to this picture. She reads it, close to the old gentleman's ear; it is a record merely of sinful thought, which never was embodied in an act; but, while Memory is reading, Conscience unveils her face, and strikes a dagger to the heart of Mr. Smith. Though not a death-blow, the torture was extreme.

The exhibition proceeded. One after another, Fancy displayed her pictures, all of which appeared to have been painted by some malicious artist, on purpose to vex Mr. Smith. Not a shadow of proof could have been adduced, in any earthly court, that he was guilty of the slightest of those sins which were thus made to stare him in the face. In one scene, there was a table set out, with several bottles, and glasses half filled with wine, which threw back the dull ray of an expiring lamp. There had been mirth and revelry, until the hand of the clock stood just at midnight, when Murder stept between the boon-companions. A young man had fallen on the floor, and lay stone dead, with a ghastly wound crushed into his temple, while over him, with a delirium of mingled rage and horror in his countenance, stood the youthful likeness of Mr. Smith. The murdered youth wore the features of Edward Spencer! 'What does this rascal of a painter mean?' cries Mr. Smith, provoked beyond all patience. 'Edward Spencer was my earliest and dearest friend, true to me as I to him, through more than half a century. Neither I, nor any other, ever murdered him. Was he not alive within five years, and did he not, in token of our long friendship, bequeath me his gold-headed cane, and a mourning ring?' Again had Memory been turning over her volume, and fixed at length upon so confused a page, that she surely must have scribbled it when she was tipsy. The purport was, however, that, while Mr. Smith and Edward Spencer were heating their young blood with wine, a quarrel had flashed up between them, and Mr. Smith, in deadly wrath, had flung a bottle at Spencer's head. True, it missed its aim, and merely smashed a looking-glass; and the next morning, when the incident was imperfectly remembered, they had shaken hands with a hearty laugh. Yet, again, while Memory was reading, Conscience unveiled her face, struck a dagger to the heart of Mr. Smith, and quelled his remonstrance with her iron frown. The pain was quite excruciating.

Some of the pictures had been painted with so doubtful a touch, and in colors so faint and pale, that the subjects could barely be conjectured. A dull, semi-transparent mist had been thrown over the surface of the canvass, into which the figures seemed to vanish, while the eye sought most earnestly to fix them. But, in every scene, however dubiously portrayed, Mr. Smith was invariably haunted by his own lineaments, at various ages, as in a dusty mirror. After poring several minutes over one of these blurred and almost indistinguishable pictures, he began to see, that the painter had intended to represent him, now in the decline of life, as stripping the clothes from the backs of three half-starved children. 'Really, this puzzles me!' quoth Mr. Smith, with the irony of conscious rectitude. 'Asking pardon of the painter, I pronounce him a fool, as well as a scandalous knave. A man of my standing in the world, to be robbing little children of their clothes! Ridiculous!'—But while he spoke, Memory had searched her fatal volume, and found a page, which, with her sad, calm voice, she poured into his ear. It was not altogether inapplicable to the misty scene. It told how Mr. Smith had been grievously tempted, by many devilish sophistries, on the ground of a legal quibble, to commence a law-suit against three orphan children, joint heirs to a considerable estate. Fortunately, before he was quite decided, his claims had turned out nearly as devoid of law, as justice. As Memory ceased to read, Conscience again thrust aside her mantle, and would have struck her victim with the envenomed dagger, only that he struggled, and clasped his hands before his heart. Even then, however, he sustained an ugly gash.

Why should we follow Fancy through the whole series of those awful pictures? Painted by an artist of wondrous power, and terrible acquaintance with the secret soul, they embodied the ghosts of all the never perpetrated sins, that had glided through the life-time of Mr. Smith. And could such beings of cloudy fantasy, so near akin to nothingness, give valid evidence against him, at the day of judgment? Be that the case or not, there is reason to believe, that one truly penitential tear would have washed away each hateful picture, and left the canvass white as snow. But Mr. Smith, at a prick of Conscience too keen to be endured, bellowed aloud, with impatient agony, and suddenly discovered that his three guests were gone. There he sat alone, a silver-haired and highly venerated old man, in the rich gloom of the crimson-curtained room, with no box of pictures on the table, but only a decanter of most excellent Madeira. Yet his heart still seemed to fester with the venom of the dagger.

Nevertheless, the unfortunate old gentleman might have argued the matter with Conscience, and alleged many reasons wherefore she should not smite him so pitilessly. Were we to take up his cause, it should be somewhat in the following fashion. A scheme of guilt, till it be put in execution, greatly resembles a train of incidents in a projected tale. The latter, in order to produce a sense of reality in the reader's mind, must be conceived with such proportionate strength by the author as to seem, in the glow of fancy, more like truth, past, present, or to come, than purely fiction. The prospective sinner, on the other hand, weaves his plot of crime, but seldom or never feels a perfect certainty that it will be executed. There is a dreaminess diffused about his thoughts; in a dream, as it were, he strikes the death-blow into his victim's heart, and starts to find an indelible blood-stain on his hand. Thus a novel-writer, or a dramatist, in creating a villain of romance, and fitting him with evil deeds, and the villain of actual life, in projecting crimes that will be perpetrated, may almost meet each other, half-way between reality and fancy. It is not until the crime is accomplished, that guilt clenches its gripe upon the guilty heart and claims it for its own. Then, and not before, sin is actually felt and acknowledged, and, if unaccompanied by repentance, grows a thousand fold more virulent by its self-consciousness. Be it considered, also, that men often over-estimate their capacity for evil. At a distance, while its attendant circumstances do not press upon their notice, and its results are dimly seen, they can bear to contemplate it. They may take the steps which lead to crime, impelled by the same sort of mental action as in working out a mathematical problem, yet be powerless with compunction, at the final moment. They knew not what deed it was, that they deemed themselves resolved to do. In truth, there is no such thing in man's nature, as a settled and full resolve, either for good or evil, except at the very moment of execution. Let us hope, therefore, that all the dreadful consequences of sin will not be incurred, unless the act have set its seal upon the thought.

Yet, with the slight fancy-work which we have framed, some sad and awful truths are interwoven. Man must not disclaim his brotherhood, even with the guiltiest, since, though his hand be clean, his heart has surely been polluted by the flitting phantoms of iniquity. He must feel, that, when he shall knock at the gate of Heaven, no semblance of an unspotted life can entitle him to entrance there. Penitence must kneel, and Mercy come from the footstool of the throne, or that golden gate will never open!

CORPORATE MEMBERS

The Peabody Essex Museum is very grateful to the following corporate members for their generous support.

PRESIDENT'S CIRCLE

Borough of Ota, Tokyo, Japan

CORPORATE PARTNERS

A. J. Callahan & Sons, Inc., Beverly Farms
Beverly National Bank, Beverly
Brewer & Lord, Braintree
Brown, Rudnick, Freed, & Gesmer, P.C., Boston
Cricket Press, Inc., Manchester
Eastern Bank, Lynn
Holyoke Mutual Insurance Co., Salem
Marblehead Savings Bank, Marblehead
OSRAM Sylvania, Inc., Danvers
The Salem Evening News, Salem
Salem Five Cents Savings Bank, Salem
Salem Oil & Grease Co., Salem
Shawmut Bank, N.A., Salem
Shetland Properties, Salem

CORPORATE BENEFACTORS

Bank of Boston, Boston
Bursaw Oil Corporation, Danvers
Connell Limited Partnership, Boston
Connolly Brothers, Inc., Beverly
DBL Printers, North Andover
J. Donovan Associates, Inc., Salem
Eastman Gelatine Corporation, Peabody
EG & G, Inc., Salem
Heritage Cooperative Bank, Salem
Hunneman Corp., Boston
IBM Corporation, Boston
King's Grant Inn, Danvers
Lotus Gifts, Salem
Parker Brothers, Beverly
George Peabody Co-operative Bank, Peabody
Raytheon Company, Lexington
Regnante, Regnante, Sterio & Osborne, Peabody
Rich's Department Store, Salem
Scott Oil Company, Manchester
Serafini, Serafini, & Darling, Salem
John Smidt Company, Inc., Peabody
WGBH Educational Foundation, Boston

CORPORATE PATRONS

Acadia Management Co., Inc., Boston
The American Marine Model Gallery, Inc., Salem
Atwood & Morrill Co., Inc., Salem
Berkal, Stelman, Davern & Shribman, Salem
Booma Oil Company, Lynn
The Boston Shipping Assoc., Inc, Boston
Brush Fibers, Inc., Salem
Cabot LNG Corp., Boston
Clarke Brothers, Inc., Salem
P. Clayman & Sons, Inc., Salem
Conrad Dental Office, Salem
Culinary Fare, Nahant
Danvers Motor Company, Danvers
Delande's Supply Co., Inc., Salem
Dinsmore Gruhl & Company, P.C., Salem
Essex Alarm & Security, Beverly
Essex Office, Inc., Salem
First Colonial Bank of Savings, Lynn
Fisher & George Electrical Company, Beverly
Fishery Products, Inc., Danvers
Harbor Sweets, Inc., Salem
Hawthorne Hotel, Salem
Hi-Da-Way Plant Branch, Inc., Salem
Hobbs Endeavour Corporation, Swampscott
Issues Management, Inc., Boston
Kallmann, McKinnell & Wood Architects, Boston
Kayem Foods, Inc., Chelsea
Kona Corporation, Gloucester
F. Kelley Landolphi, Attorney, Salem
Ledoux, Whipple & King, P.C., Salem
Arthur D. Little, Inc., Cambridge
McDougall Associates, Inc., Peabody
National Grand Bank, Marblehead
The Nimrod Press, Boston
North Shore Weeklies, Ipswich
Northshore International Insurance Services, Inc., Salem
Amelia Payson Guest House, Salem
Pickering Wharf Marina, Salem
Precision Connector Designs, Inc., Peabody

OF THE PEABODY ESSEX MUSEUM

Ryan & Coscia, P.C., Salem
Salem Interiors, Salem
Salem State College, Salem
Soucy Insurance Agency, Inc., Salem
Stahl Associates Ltd., Boston
Tinti, Quinn, & Savoy, Salem
Van Waters & Rogers, Inc., Salem
Waters & Brown, Inc., Salem
West Lynn Creamery, Lynn
Witch Dungeon Museum, Inc., Salem

CORPORATE SPONSORS

T. E. Andresen Moving & Storage, Salem
Ardiff & Morse, P.C., Danvers
Art Supplies Wholesale, Beverly
Augustine's Restaurant, Saugus
Barlow Designs, Inc., Rhode Island
Peter D. Barter Flowers, Salem
Bartlett Tree Experts, Beverly Farms
Bear Leigh of Bearksin Neck, Rockport
Bernard's Jewelers, Salem
A. Berube and Son, Inc., Salem
The Beverly Times, Beverly
Blair House Antiques, Beverly
Bond Leather Co., Inc., Peabody
Paul Boucher Masonry, Salem
Bostik Incorporated, Middleton
Broad Street Trust, Lynn
Cape Ann Tree and Landscape, Magnolia
Cappuccio Liquors, Salem
Carr Leather Company, Lynn
William Charles Studio, Salem
Ted Cole's Music Shop, Salem
F. L. Conway and Sons Funeral Home, Peabody
2nd Corps Cadets Veterans Assoc., Peabody
Country Curtains, Stockbridge
Elizabeth Creed & Company, Ltd., Beverly
Crosby's Market Place, Salem
Danvers Savings Bank, Danvers
DeIulis Brothers Construction Co., Lynn
Delux Corporation Foundation, Framingham
Endicott College, Beverly
Entertainment Northeast, Boston
Farm Creek Landscaping, Inc., Gloucester
Galacar & Company, Essex
Grantham, Mayo Van Otterloo & Co., Boston
Griffin Pension Services, Inc., South Hamilton
Gulf of Maine Research Center, Inc., Salem
Happy Hands, Newburyport
Honey Baked Ham Co., Marblehead
Ice House Marketplace, Newburyport
The Inn at Seven Winter Street, Salem
J. D. Custom Woodworking, Peabody
Kaminski Auctioneers & Appraisers, Stoneham
W. J. Mayer & Company, Greenwich, CT
Krikorian Miller Associates, Newburyport
Everett Mills Real Estate, Lawrence
Daniel Low & Company, Salem
Lyceum Bar & Grill, Salem
Mingo Gallery Inc., Beverly
Minit-Print, Salem
N & D Cleaning Company, Salem
New England Telephone, Wakefield
North Bennet Street School, Boston
Old Naumkeag Antiques, Salem
Omni Products, Boxford
Pro Creations, Southborough
L. H. Rogers, Inc., Salem
The Russian Gallery, Marblehead
St. John's Preparatory School, Danvers
The Salem Inn, Salem
Salem Witch Museum, Salem
Sapient Corporation, Cambridge
Schylling Associates, Inc., Essex
Shearson, Lehman Brothers, Peabody
Sherman & Epstein, CPA, Peabody
Sotheby's Inc., Boston
The Stinehour Press, Vermont
Tri-City Sales, Inc., Salem

IN MEMORIAM

Nina Fletcher Little

1903–1993

A Member of the
Board of Editors of the
Essex Institute Historical Collections